THE YOUNG SHOT

N. M. SEDGWICK

The Young
Shot

THIRD EDITION

ADAM & CHARLES BLACK
LONDON

FIRST PUBLISHED 1940
REPRINTED 1944 AND 1951
SECOND EDITION 1958
REPRINTED 1961, 1964 AND 1969
THIRD EDITION 1975

A. & C. BLACK LTD
4, 5 AND 6 SOHO SQUARE, LONDON W1V 6AD

© A. & C. Black Ltd
ISBN 0 7136 1609 1

PRINTED AND BOUND IN GREAT BRITAIN BY
MORRISON AND GIBB LTD., LONDON AND EDINBURGH

CONTENTS

CONTENTS

CONTENTS

ILLUSTRATIONS

Photographs

Drawings in the text

ACKNOWLEDGMENTS

GRATEFULLY I acknowledge my indebtedness to those friends who have so kindly allowed me to use photographs taken by themselves to illustrate this volume; to Mr. G. K. Yeates; to Mr. R. Clapham; to Mr. J. Ritchie; to Mr. Stanley Duncan; to Mr. T. D. S. Purdey and Captain J. A. Purdey for the illustration on page 23 from their excellent book *The Shot Gun*; also to the *Shooting Times and British Sportsman* and to the *Illustrated Sporting and Dramatic News* for allowing me to reproduce photographs that have appeared in those journals. I am also indebted to my old friend Mr. Frank Redmond for the use of photographs, in which he appears, taken at a shooting school, and last, but not least to my friends Mr. E. F. Cross and Captain W. H. T. Long for " vetting " the chapter " Guns and Cartridges."

PREFACE

WHEN I wrote this book in 1940, there was no indication
of three "events" approaching which were to shake
the world of sport—namely, the Government's decision to
ban the steel trap (gin) in July 1958, the passing of the Wild
Birds Protection Act 1954, and the spread of that foul disease,
myxomatosis. The banning of the steel trap, of course, has set
a problem to rabbit-trappers, and all those who trap ground
vermin such as stoats, weasels, rats, etc. True, the Government
have chosen certain designs for "humane" traps which will be
legal, these traps killing the victim outright, though it is obvious
to any practical trapper or keeper that they will never again
have such an efficient, all-round trap as the common gin.

When I was asked to revise this book at the end of 1957,
I realized at once that my chapters on trapping rabbits and
smaller vermin had become (or soon would become) redundant,
but my publishers agreed with me that the Young Shot of the
future should know something about conditions of looking
after game in the past, and that therefore I should leave the
chapters concerned untouched, explaining the change-over to
humane traps in this Foreword.

PREFACE TO THE THIRD EDITION

MODERN SHOOTING TECHNIQUES

THIS book was first published in 1940 when N. M. Sedgwick was no longer young. He and his generation habitually used a method of shooting, a technique of handling a gun, which is now called " lead-and-swing". It was the only means of coping with flying targets in the days of the flint-lock and it still has merit; but it would be quite wrong to believe that it is the one effective way of using a modern gun. To do so would be to deny the value of all the advances made in this century.

Quite where, or when, the new methods were born is uncertain but Robert Churchill, the gunmaker, was teaching his, then revolutionary, technique in 1931. His book, *Game Shooting*, first published in 1955 by Michael Joseph, describes his methods.

Percy Stanbury, an outstanding shot and for many years an instructor at the West London Shooting Grounds, held different views. His style is so distinctive that his pupils can be recognized at a distance. He has written three books in collaboration with G. L. Carlisle, *Shotgun Markmanship*, *Clay Pigeon Marksmanship* and *Shotgun and Shooter* (Barrie & Jenkins).

My own *Shooting Game* (A. & C. Black) and J. E. M. Ruffer's *The Art of Good Shooting* (David & Charles) were published more recently. Both add something new and it is reasonable to suppose that the future will see further advances.

All these methods have their powers and their limitations; it would be foolish to maintain that there is but one true doctrine and that all else is heresy. A perfect shot would master all techniques and any novice who confined himself to that described in this book would be handicapped.

TRAPPING AND SNARING

In a perfect world there would be neither traps nor snares. Species harmful to man would be controlled cheaply, easily and, above all, painlessly by better means. Unhappily we have not yet reached that state although some progress has been made since *The Young Shot* was first published.

The cruel gin-trap referred to in the text has been illegal since 1958. Trapping rabbits is a thing of the past; so, almost entirely, is the trapping of rats; and setting snares for either is unnecessary. More humane methods of control are now available, and that they are cheaper, quicker, demand less skill and are more effective is all to the good.

No substitute for traps as a defence against mink, stoats, weasels and grey squirrels has yet been discovered but, and this is a great step forward, traps which kill these small creatures instantly are now available. The Fenn trap and the Sawyer and Lloyd traps are examples of " humane " types but others exist. It is now illegal to set such traps outside a tunnel or burrow. To put them on poles, in nests, under water, in the open or any where at all except in a tunnel or burrow is to break the law. In fact the only traps which may be set in any other place are cages and box-traps, which are tunnels in themselves.

Moles are still trapped occasionally but the usual method of control involves poison.

The use of snares is only tolerated because they provide the one effective, legal means of dealing with foxes and the occasional rogue badger. Even so they should be treated as weapons of last resort and held in reserve until more humane methods have proved inadequate.

Every trap and snare must be visited every day; the law

and common humanity demands it; but snares should be inspected twice, preferably at dawn and at sunset.

It might well be asked why the sections of this book which describe trapping and snaring are retained since they may spread knowledge of things which are both illegal and cruel, but there are other considerations. Apart from their interest as a record of bygone methods they contain much that is still valuable. For instance everything concerning the siting of tunnels is as true today as ever: the substitution of a Fenn trap for a gin is the only difference.

Moreover the author has caught the atmosphere. He makes plain that no matter how greatly traps are to be deplored they are indispensable; and, once the necessity has been accepted, they result in a fascinating battle of wits between the trapper and the evil-doer. A good trapper must be more than something of a naturalist; he must make a close study of his opponents.

It is also possible that some of the discarded methods will be revived in the future. Rats present few problems at present because they succumb so easily to Warfarin; but if a strain of rats immune to such poisons were evolved—and it has happened in small areas—knowledge of how to trap and snare them would be sorely needed.

In the same way the art of taking protected birds should remain dormant rather than be lost. At present all the falcons, hawks and owls are protected by law, and rightly so. If sparrowhawks, however, proliferated as the woodpigeon has done the law would be changed and the old skills would be called upon to defend the finches.

FERRETING

Ferrets are still kept and used in the manner described in Chapter Ten, but their rôle has changed. They were once working animals; the only means by which rats and rabbits

PREFACE

which had taken refuge in burrows could be controlled; but now that Cymag completes that task more easily ferrets are seldom used except for sport.

The Protection of Birds Acts 1954 and 1967.

Many birds which are habitually shot when this book was first published are now protected by law. A layman's guide to these Acts will be found in Appendix One.

MICHAEL KEMP.

Game Shooting Seasons

(All dates inclusive)

Grouse .	. Aug. 12 – Dec. 10
Blackgame	. Aug. 20 – Dec. 10
Ptarmigan	. Aug. 12 – Dec. 10
Partridge	. Sept. 1 – Feb. 1
Pheasant	. Oct. 1 – Feb. 1
Snipe .	. Aug. 12 – Jan. 31
Woodcock	. Sept. 1 – Jan. 31 (Scotland)
Woodcock	. Oct. 1 – Jan. 31 (England and Wales)
Wildfowl	. Sept. 1 – Feb. 20 (in or over areas below the high-water mark of ordinary spring tides).
Wildfowl	. Sept. 1 – Jan. 31 (elsewhere)

SHOTGUN CERTIFICATES AND GAME LICENCES

Gun Licences have now been abolished and Shotgun Certificates have replaced them. It is illegal to possess a shotgun without a Shotgun Certificate. These certificates are issued by the police, are valid for three years and cost 75 pence. Application forms can be obtained at police stations.

I

GAME AND GUN LICENCES

No certificate is required for an airgun or air-rifle.

Game Licences can be obtained from Post Offices. The charges are:—

For one year expiring July 31	£6.00
From August to October 31 or from November to July 31	£4.00
Any period of 14 consecutive days	£2.00
A gamekeeper's licence for one year	£4.00

It is illegal to " take " game without a game licence, and " taking " includes shooting, netting, trapping and snaring. One who assists in the " taking " of game also requires a game licence; thus, even if he is only shooting rabbits, a man who is out with a game-shooting party must have a game licence.

Game may not be taken on Sundays or on Christmas Day.

CHAPTER ONE

Shooting To-day

*" The Old Order Changeth "—Syndicate Shoots—Early
Tuition — In the Keeper's Charge — The Value of
Shooting-Schools*

IN an age when money is scarce and heavy taxation has
caused many landowners to dispose of their estates and
even their old homes ; when men have less leisure and are
forced to spend the greater part of the week earning a livelihood, the young shooter has not the same opportunities of
engaging in field sports as had his forebears.

In the days before the Great War of 1914–18 the country
boy whose inclinations and instincts leaned towards an open-
air life and those sports which were part and parcel of a rural
existence, graduated in a manner that was not only enjoyable
to himself, but which developed in him a real love for Nature
and an ever-increasing thirst for first-hand knowledge of the
wild life of the countryside.

From the time that he learned to toddle, to that long-
looked-for day when he took his place for the first time among
adults in the shooting-field, his elders saw to it that his training
as a sportsman was systematic, thorough and accomplished in
such a manner that the boy neither resented the strict enforce-
ment of sporting principles, nor wearied in a process that
would have made no appeal to a town-bred contemporary.
The father who noted with pleasure that his son showed a
natural keenness towards a country life and sport, delightedly,
but firmly, sought to instil the right spirit in his offspring,

3

encouraging him to show an interest in shooting matters at the earliest age it was possible for him to appreciate them.

Right from the start, the boy was taught that there was an ever-present danger where firearms and cartridges were concerned and the folly of treating even a toy gun or pistol merely as a toy.

How often do we learn of serious or fatal accidents occurring when a gun, thought to be empty, has been pointed at some one and the trigger pressed, when to the everlasting horror and regret of the handler, an explosion has followed with dire results. Such accidents, it may be said without fear of contradiction, would have been rare if every one who handles a gun had been brought up under the supervision of a sportsman of the old school.

Quite apart, however, from that side of shooting, concerning actual weapons and how best to handle and use them, our fathers took good care gradually to teach us all about game and other creatures of the woods and fields, pointing out from the day we became the possessor of a catapult, or our first airgun, which animals and birds might be considered legitimate quarry and which must be left well alone, however great the temptation to stalk and shoot them. Thus, for instance, in the days of my youth, the starling and the sparrow might be stalked and shot with impunity, but the hedge-sparrow, the linnets and the finches were put out of bounds, despite the damage done to fruit-trees by some of the latter. Blackbirds and thrushes, all too often a source of temptation to a boy with an airgun or a catapult as they sat in the hedgerows, were considered on the unofficial protection list, except for a period of the year when the cherries were ripe and they raided the trees. During that short time, at different ages, good practice was enjoyed, first with an air-rifle and later with a ·410, and the result was eagerly anticipated in the form of blackbird pie.

There is no doubt about it, the identification and habits of

4

the animals and birds of the countryside which comes with practice, the ability to stalk those species that are the legitimate quarry of the shooter and the restraint occasioned by the stern teaching of an older sportsman are three of the most important and useful lessons that a youthful shot can master. For it is the man who is keen to find his own game and is an adept at doing so who gets the most enjoyment out of the sport of shooting, and who becomes the envy of his fellow-sportsmen less well acquainted with shooting-field procedure and the habits and ways of wild creatures.

" The Old Order Changeth "—a fact that must be re-cognised by the young shot who has studied the writings of past generations of sportsmen and listened to the conversation of his elders anent " old times." In the first decade of this century, practically all the shooting was in individual hands. By this I mean that those who owned or rented the shooting of large estates, and even those with shallower purses who took small shoots, seldom shared the expense with others. Their shooting was their own, and they invited guests to enjoy it, themselves being invited to shoot elsewhere in return. The syndicate shoot was hardly known and, where it existed, was regarded askance and with a quiet sense of suspicion.

To-day, by reason of heavy taxation and other economic changes, all too many of our big estates have been split up, large farms have in many cases been divided into a series of small holdings and the syndicate shoot has become an estab-lished and recognised feature of sport. More than this, we now recognise syndicate shoots as a necessity, for without them probably millions of acres of ground would remain unshot, vermin would thrive and game would go to the wall.

To explain briefly the value of the syndicate shoot, let us imagine an estate of three thousand acres on which the former owner or shooting tenant killed the most satisfactory bags of pheasants, partridges, hares and rabbits. Finding that he could no longer pay the wages of three or four keepers and

5

a side of beaters in due season, shoulder the considerable expense of rearing and feeding several hundred or even thousand pheasants and entertaining his friends, he is faced with two alternatives. Either he must sack his keepers and let his shooting go to seed, or let the shooting and benefit financially by the transaction.

It is possible that the shooting may be taken over by a more fortunate individual, but it is far more likely that a syndicate of guns, either chosen by himself, or complete strangers to him, will be attracted by his offer and, if he feels inclined, he will make it a stipulation that he, himself, reserves the right to become one of the guns in the syndicate.

For the sake of argument, let us suppose that five guns form the syndicate, each paying £100. For that figure each will be entitled to enjoy the resulting sport, and will be able, on stipulated occasions, to ask a friend. He will also benefit by the sale of game, for it is usual with such shoots to share the game killed, or the profits made by the sale of such game.

My object in briefly outlining the " status " of the syndicate shoot here is this. In the old days (hackneyed expression) the young shooter, after serving his earliest apprenticeship under his father or some sporting relative, graduated to a further apprenticeship under a keeper. During the latter period, he not only continued to be shown with what care firearms must be handled, but at first hand he learned the ways of game and vermin, the best methods of pigeon shooting and rabbiting, the way to set traps and snares for the enemies of game, and many other useful items of game preservation and natural history that would stand him in good stead during future years. By the time he had spent a few holidays in the company of the keeper he had, in fact, been taught almost as much as that worthy knew himself and had learned how to " take " various shots. His keenness, if he was intelligent and had been blessed by nature with a natural facility to adapt himself to circumstances, was whetted to a fine edge. So that when

6

the day finally arrived that he took his place in the shooting-field with his elders, he was in a position to appreciate the art of putting game over the guns, and, with due deference, was able to discuss affairs with older sportsmen.

On the other hand, it must be admitted that a great number of those men who have of recent years taken up shooting and joined syndicate shoots at middle age have been more concerned with a business life than one connected with country matters. All honour to them. They have become the backbone of the shooting world, and are bringing up their sons at an early age to enjoy field sports. It must be admitted, however, that a majority of them are concerned more with the sport they enjoy than with the natural history and woodcraft side of it. Their time is limited ; they have not had the opportunity of studying every aspect of game preservation, but they are none the less keen that their sons should enter whole-heartedly into it. Unhappily, their sons are also compelled to work to make sufficient money to enjoy country recreations, and week-ends alone make it exceedingly difficult to accumulate that knowledge of wild life that was the heritage of those of a more fortunate period.

Accordingly (and while this book is written for the benefit of young shooters who are as keen as mustard to learn and spend most of their spare time enjoying field sports) I confess that during recent years I have discovered that there are three distinctive classes of shooting-men. First, those who, through the assistance of shooting-schools and constant practice concentrate on becoming proficient shots, but quite neglect to learn about the preservation and " showing " of game, the rudiments of natural history and the appreciation of environments in which they find themselves in the shooting-field. Secondly, those who have little to learn concerning game, and to whom the countryside is an open book, but who seem content to shoot badly or indifferently all their days. Thirdly, those who, successfully or unsuccessfully, strive to

7

combine those two essentials of a good sportsman and shot—
the ability to handle a gun easily and with excellent results
and a genuine appreciation and interest in everything about
them. It goes without saying that it is men of this latter type
who most enjoy the sport of shooting and are good and welcome
companions in the butts or on the rough shoot.

What advice, then, would I give to the young and
enthusiastic shot who may still be at school, and who will
eventually graduate to take his place in the world of business ?
Those of an older generation, whose paths through life were
easier than they would be to-day under existing circumstances
are apt to be too critical of youth. They say, and with truth,
that this is a mechanical age, an age when young men think
far more of sports-cars, motor-bicycles and ball games. That
the boy who is keen on field sports, who glories in the opportunity of being in the company of the keeper, who spends
many hours on his own, stalking sparrows with an air-rifle,
or walking round the fields with a shotgun, and who revels
in such night ventures as those of catching sparrows and rats
round the farm buildings and hedgerows is to-day an exception which proves a rule. Nevertheless, I look forward to a
greater interest being shown in these once popular major
and minor sports and pastimes of young countrymen, and I
believe that the new era of syndicate shoots and the resultant
keenness being shown by a rising generation in country life
will in some part bring about a revival of them, and I hope
that my own experiences related in this book may be helpful ;
perhaps even inspiring.

Shooting with an air-rifle or a miniature rifle is supposed
to hamper one in learning to become a proficient performer
with a shotgun. With the former it is necessary to take careful
and deliberate aim at a " sitting " target, while with a shotgun
a rapid decision and calculation, even as the shotgun is
mounting to the shoulder, and often the pressing of the
trigger almost at the same instant as the stock of the weapon

8

becomes comfortably "embedded," is necessary when shooting at moving objects. Thus it is said that the young sportsman, hitherto acquainted only with a rifle, finds himself "slow" with a shotgun on getting on to the mark while making rapid mental calculations concerning the speed and angle of a moving target—calculations that later, with practice, become almost automatic in a good shot. In fact, I have known a sporting parent deny his son the use of air-rifle or rifle for this very reason, but I consider his view very short-sighted indeed.

Not only does sport with an air-rifle teach a beginner the necessity for faithfulness of aim, but it shows him that before aim can be taken his quarry has often to be stalked to bring it within range. And the quarry cannot always be successfully stalked unless the stalker has a very fair knowledge of its habits and characteristics. The boy who has spent several years or even months enjoying sport with an air-rifle becomes proficient in the art of finding his quarry, identifying it by its "mannerisms," stalking to within range and finally bringing it to bag with an accurately placed slug. In this performance we view the advancing shadow of a practical sportsman who will be good at finding his own game, will take a great interest in everything appertaining to sport and who, as likely as not, is a good shot.

Compare a boy of this kind with one who, after a few lessons at a shooting school, is handed a shotgun and let loose, as it were, on a rough shoot. The former will immediately feel at home, and his alert and partly trained senses will stand him in good stead. The latter, on the other hand, will be at a loss how to proceed and even should he stumble upon game, will probably be taken by surprise, and his shooting-school training will only be remembered when the game has departed out of shot, or even out of sight.

My advice, then, to those young shots who have not the opportunity of being brought up in a country home under the tuition of a sporting parent, but who are keen at heart

9

to become good sportsmen and good shots, is this. Get in as much " work " as possible in the early days with an accurate air-rifle, meanwhile studying the identification and habits of wild creatures. There are many excellent books and a few papers devoted to field sports which will not only prove of considerable value in this latter respect, but will whet the appetite for further knowledge. When the day arrives that it is considered that a shotgun of small bore may take the place of the air-rifle, the pupil should pay a visit to a gunmaker or to a shooting-school, where he will be " fitted " for his gun, a subject of importance that will be dealt with in another chapter.

Of the modern shooting school I cannot give a better description than that outlined by my friend, Captain J. B. Drought, in his *A Shot in the Making*. He says :

" (i) It minimises the likelihood of acquiring bad habits, because from the outset, errors in weapon-handling, stance and footwork are detected and the reasons why and wherefore are explained in simple language.

" (ii) The range and penetrating power of guns can be accurately gauged by the keen and so far inexperienced observer.

" (iii) The heights and angles at which clay pigeons are shown, as well as their lengths of flight enable the novice to see for himself what leads are applicable to driven birds under varying conditions.

" (iv) Instruction is gradual. For example, the ' right and left ' comes as a sequel to, and not concomitant with, the practice of walking-up single birds.

" (v) A shot is no sooner fired than its exact position in relation to the object is detected by the expert eye, and the reason for missing high or low, to the right or left, is explained.

" (vi) The practice ground resembles the shooting-field, as far as human ingenuity can contrive. In fields of natural scrub and bushes there are concealed a variety of traps, one of which will send a clay 'rabbit' scuttling along a ride while another pushes out a skimming partridge. There are single and double rises of grouse and partridges driven over butts and hedges, and from behind a belt of tall elms pheasants come whizzing from the top of a tower. So that while every type of shot likely to be encountered later on by the embryo marksman in the field is shown him under artificial conditions, a point of supreme importance to my mind is this : he sees the various ways in which game presents itself to the gun, and the heights at which the different species fly, and whether he is walking up the rough stuff, standing behind a low hedge or waiting in the open for high pheasants, the least intelligent youth should grasp the margin of safety in respect of his fellow creatures requisite in all circumstances. If he does not, the instructor at his elbow will very quickly put him wise to what is or is not a risky shot."

Briefly, then—very briefly indeed, I fear—I have attempted to show how times and opportunities have changed and under what advantages and handicaps the young shot of to-day is brought up to the etiquette and facts of the shooting-field. It now remains for me, in the space of a single volume, to offer what help I can to the tyro whose heart is set to become a keen and accomplished sportsman and one whose reputation as such, and especially as a safe shot, will earn for him not only the respect of fellow sportsmen, from contemporaries to those of advanced years, but also invitations to shoot from all and sundry — invitations, moreover, readily and gladly made, the outcome of his own prowess with the gun and a popularity born of knowledge and experience well applied.

CHAPTER TWO

Safety First

Gun Accidents—Rudimentary Precautions—Carrying a Gun—Negotiating Ditches and Fences—Risky Shooting a Crime—A Warning.

A PARTY of four guns had been enjoying an afternoon and evening's sport on a sewage farm. During the afternoon, we had accounted for a few pheasants and eight couple of snipe, and, as it grew dusk, duck arrived from several lakes and ponds, and we shot and collected about a dozen. When it was too dark for further shooting, the bag was divided, the dogs whistled up (they were in a fine pickle), and we headed for the neighbouring town where the cars had been left. Later, two of us entered a local inn, for " a crust of bread and cheese " and to yarn over the events of the expedition. Guns were left in the corner of the taproom and dogs kennelled in a shed in the yard. Presently there entered one or two more men who had also been flighting duck, and three guns were added to the " armoury " in the corner. Half an hour later we decided to start for home, and to this day it is difficult to say how the accident occurred. A stranger present who had been discussing guns, picked up one belonging to the last party to enter and was examining it, when a roar like an exploding mine left us all dazed. Somehow the gun had gone off, and the charge of shot had torn a big hole in the ceiling of the room. Try to imagine the feelings of those present ; of the man who had left his gun loaded ; of him who had inadvertently caused the accident.   It were better, perhaps, to draw a curtain over the scene.

Again, a farmer of my acquaintance, as a rule a very careful shot, was shooting ferreted rabbits, and a lad of sixteen was working the ferrets.   Two rabbits had bolted and been shot from a burrow in the bank of a deep ditch, and when what the farmer took to be a third rabbit was seen moving on the top of the bank a yard or two from the hole, he raised his gun and fired.   Unfortunately, the boy had run along the bottom of the ditch to pick up a ferret; as he stood upright, the top of his head just showed through some brambles over the bank.   It was this at which the farmer fired, and the boy was killed instantly.   That farmer parted with his guns and vowed never to shoot again—a vow he has kept to this day.

Only a short time ago, a friend of mine was shot dead as his companion handed him a loaded gun from a car, and his wife who was present and witnessed the accident, still suffers from shock.

There are many other accidents, fatal and serious, that I could quote, which though of the kind known as " accidental " would undoubtedly have been avoided had the elementary rules of " Safety First " been observed, and the gun regarded in the light of a lethal weapon, rather than as a familiar weapon of sport.

As a boy of nine, I once had occasion to suffer badly from a sense of injustice.   In play, I was seen by my father, a sportsman of the old school, to point a stick at a companion. I was not only severely reprimanded, but the inoffensive (in my eyes) weapon descended several times upon a fleshy portion of my anatomy, causing me considerable physical and mental anguish.   " What harm could there be," I asked myself, " in pointing a stick in play?   For once my father was in the wrong and I would let him see that I knew this in my own way ! "   I now know that my father was perfectly right, and if his method of correction was a little drastic, it put me on the right line—that line of subconscious thought that automatically encourages the greatest care when handling a dangerous weapon.

If you get into the habit, innocently enough, of pointing a stick in play, you may presently point a toy gun in the same manner. Later, still with no thought of dangerous practice, an unloaded air-rifle, rifle, or shotgun may be aimed in fun, when, due to a slip of the memory or to the carelessness of some one else, it will be discovered too late that the unloaded weapon was, in fact, not unloaded, and a terrible accident results.

One has only to read newspaper reports of such accidents over the course of a year, to realise the extent to which they occur. And by no means every accident of this kind finds its way into print.

A gun should always be treated as if it were loaded. By this I mean that at no time should it be pointed, deliberately, or through careless handling, at man or dog. It should never be laid down, or leant against an object until it has been " broken " to ascertain that it is empty. Likewise, a gun must not be taken into a car or into the house until the same precautions have been taken. It is not enough to *think* the cartridges have been extracted, or to rely on fickle memory. Always, without exception, " break " the weapon under those and similar conditions outlined, and it is as well to make a habit of looking through the barrels, just to ascertain for certain that no obstruction exists.

To treat a gun as unloaded that is merely uncocked, or on " safe " is as much a crime as to leave the cartridges in it. Many a gun on " safe " left standing against a wall has been knocked down by a passing man or dog, and, the hammer coming into contact with the ground, has forced the striking-pin against the cap, with obvious results. On other occasions, hammerless guns have been known to fire under similar conditions because, even if the safety catch is at " safe " an impact may dislodge the restraining mechanism so that the tumbler falls and fires the gun.

Gun accidents happen in many unexpected ways, and for this reason no precautions taken in the interests of safety should be overlooked.

It is a simple matter for a twig to catch in the trigger as the shooter is pushing his way through thick cover, or between, say, trees of the description of the larch. Again, it is not unduly rare for a sleeve or coat button to become entangled with the trigger. For this reason, a gun should always be uncocked, or on " safe " while walking through woods and undergrowth, or over rough ground where a faulty step may cause a fall.

Actually there are two schools of thought concerning the carrying of a gun when game shooting, even over flat ground. The first definitely asserts that a gun should never be carried unless it is on " safe " and that this in no way hinders quick shooting at rising game, since the safety-catch may be automatically slipped up with the thumb as the gun is brought to the shoulder. If this method is practised, the two movements become one, and there is obviated the risk of pulling the trigger, only to find that one has forgotten to cock the gun.

The second school insists that over reasonably flat and firm ground it is perfectly safe to carry the gun at " full cock," and that one can shoot quicker and with a clearer mind if one does not have to remember to slip up the safety-catch. It is argued that this movement may be overlooked, in spite of habit, more often than one would omit to cock his gun. I must here confess that since I was brought up (with a hammer gun) under the second system, I have always stuck to it, since I feared it would be some time before the habit of slipping up the safety-catch as the gun approaches the shoulder could be acquired. Consequently, I sin in the eyes of those of the first school of thought, while theoretically agreeing with their principles. I would, in fact, impress on beginners the wisdom of acquiring the habit of walking, even on firm going, with the gun on " safe."

A major crime of the shooting-field is that of climbing a gate, a fence, a wall, or a stile, with a loaded gun. And equally does this apply to crossing a ditch, getting through wire, or forcing a way through a gap in the fence. It is not enough, when so doing, to put the gun on " safe," or even to " break " it, as is so often the custom. The weapon should be " broken " and the cartridges extracted, and there is no excuse for not doing so. Maybe a covey will rise as one clambers through a hedge, or climbs a gate with unloaded gun, but far better that such should occur and the game depart unshot at, than that neglect of these precautions should bring about an accident.

There are only two right ways of carrying a gun, one being under the arm with the barrels pointing towards the ground; the other, over the shoulder with the trigger-guard upwards. With the barrels thus pointing skywards, they can never swing into line with some one's head, even a man far taller than the carrier.

There is an old saying that mud sticks, and I think this is most applicable when it refers to a boy or a man who either on occasion, or as a habit, is known to take risky shots, or to carry or handle a gun in a manner that makes other members of the party feel uneasy for their safety. It is said also that punishment should fit the crime, and the obvious punishment for carelessness in gun-handling or shooting is not only to gain the unenviable reputation of being dangerous, but to find that one is not included in invitations to shoot.

I suppose it is only natural that a boy is almost expected to behave shall we say rashly? in the shooting-field, and for this reason his elders will keep a weather eye on him, particularly if he is standing, or walking, as " next gun." Such a supposition is not altogether unreasonable, and happily when we are young and keen we are often oblivious of facts that might otherwise make us feel self-conscious.

Yet what a wonderful opportunity a day in the shooting-field with his elders opens out to a boy who already appreciates the value of " safety first " methods. Watching him expectantly, older guns may find with pleasant surprise that the tyro in their midst is behaving like " an old sportsman," and it may be seen also that, in fact, certain older members of the party might well take useful lessons from this youthful performer. Such a boy not only becomes the subject of gunroom gossip, but he will find that he will be included in all sorts of shooting invitations, in some cases as a mark of esteem by elders who wish to show their appreciation of his conduct in some material form.

There are many forms of dangerous shooting that may be considered common, and which should be avoided at all costs.

When beaters are approaching in covert, however tempting may be the desire to shoot in their direction, it is little short of criminal folly to do so. For one thing, it is difficult to judge by voices and stick-tappings the exact distance of the beating line, while it should be remembered that the line is seldom kept where undergrowth is dense, and that though the voices of several beaters may be heard approaching at some distance, there may be other and quieter beaters much closer. Particularly are young beaters inclined to get out of line and where rabbits are plentiful and add to their excitement, there is no telling how far these youngsters have erred from their proper positions.

Should you be a " walking gun " (*i.e.* detailed off to walk outside the covert in line with the beaters) the foregoing warnings are even more necessary, for beaters have a habit

C   17

of running back, or forward, in pursuit of wounded game or rabbits, and a shot fired forward of, or behind, the line may well be the means of peppering or seriously wounding one of the beating side.

No game bird that ever flew, no hare or rabbit that was ever born in burrow or form is worth a risky shot, although it will be found that rabbit shooting in covert is often carried on in a manner that makes the safe shot wish that he had stayed at home.

Perhaps the most dangerous kind of shooting is that when some guns line a ride in the wood while others, acting as shooting-beaters, drive the game towards them. When this form of shooting is necessary (and there is no denying the fact that it is a very successful and popular method of killing rabbits in covert) it is essential that the beating guns keep strictly in line and walk slowly through the wood. Even so, it must not be taken for granted that a perfect line is kept. Perhaps a member of the party will run back for a wounded rabbit, when he instantly places himself in a dangerous position. If he finds it necessary to retrieve something he has shot, he should call out to the rest of the line to halt while he does so. If dogs accompany the line and are allowed to hunt, or retrieve dead or wounded game, the very greatest care must be exercised not to shoot where visibility is bad, or at rabbits being chased closely by dogs. It has been my sad lot to see several valuable and devoted dogs killed under these circumstances by careless shooting, and one has only to imagine the feelings of a gun who causes the death of a friend's dog to realise the foolishness of risky shooting.

"Never shoot where you can't see" is an invaluable rule and one which also applies to comparatively open country where some innocent labourer may be eating his lunch behind a hedge, or a passer-by, or horses, cattle and sheep may be hidden behind trees or bushes. Never take a chance, however remote—or the rest of your shooting life may be clouded

18

by the remembrance of a fatal or serious accident caused by
you in a moment of rashness. And don't forget—mud sticks.
Guns lining a ride must not shoot in front unless beating guns
are still far away. Rabbits are best shot after they have passed
across the ride, for they may be followed by dogs well ahead
of the beating guns. For this reason, a stand should be chosen,
where possible, that allows of clear shooting in the rear.
Here, again, no gun should move from his stand to retrieve
game until the drive is over. If he does so, long before the
walking guns come within range, he must let his fellow-guns
along the ride know of his intentions. On no account must
rabbits be shot as they cross the ride, or even followed by the
barrels of the gun, or guns standing in that direction will be
placed in danger.

" Follow not across the line " runs another old and
valuable rule, and one which deserves as much prominence
as any as a warning to young shooters. To illustrate exactly
what this infers, let us take a line of guns at a partridge shoot,
waiting at their appointed stands a few yards behind a low
hedge. On the far side of the hedge the ground may rise or
be flat, so that it is possible to take your birds well in front
—fine oncoming shots that should be taken in preference to
the common habit of allowing birds to pass before shooting
after their tails. If they are not taken out in front of the
stand, then the shooter, who has obviously proved himself
" slow on the uptake," is apt to swing his gun with the covey
so that it is either discharged down the line of stands, to the
grave danger and righteous indignation of the members of
the party concerned, or its passage across the line will badly
shake their nerves and may well earn a severe and well-
deserved reprimand. So never, never shoot down the line, or
follow through it with your barrels. If a chance of taking
birds in front has been missed, lower the barrels of the gun
as you turn to shoot at the departing covey and raise them
again only as you face the rear of the line. Remember, also,

that to shoot at birds at an acute angle in front of the line may result in pellets ricochetting off stones, or even off the plumage of the birds themselves, and striking the hedge behind which the stands are placed, or a fellow-gun.

To sum up: " Safety First " must be the motto of all sportsmen—a motto that must lie blazoned across the mind at all times where a lethal weapon is concerned. To ensure that such is the case, never forget to remove the cartridges from your gun when climbing a gate or fence, when pushing through a gap, or springing over an open drain. Never take a loaded gun into a car or into a building, and never place one down even if you are shooting on your own. Precautions of this kind may not appear so necessary when no one is present, but they are nevertheless just as important, for bad habits of this kind may be subconsciously repeated when in the company of other guns, and there is always the chance of a dog, or even the wind causing a loaded gun propped against wall or fence to tumble to the ground.

It is not enough, I repeat, that a weapon be treated as unloaded just because the hammers are down, or because it is on " safe." Shoot only where you can be assured that " the coast is clear " ; never take even a minor risk. Walking with a loaded or an empty gun, remember always to see that the barrels are pointed earthwards, or towards the sky, and never swing across the line of a companion. When loading a weapon, slip the cartridges into the breech and bring the stock of the gun upwards to the barrels, and not the barrels upwards to the stock, for then they are pointing away from the direct vicinity of the ground and should the gun be discharged for any reason, the charge of shot will fly wide.

Remember, too, that when carrying an empty gun carelessly, you may be aware of its safety, but that your neighbour may be in grave doubt and his nerves suffer accordingly. On several occasions I have seen a careful shot go over to a fellow-gun who has been walking in line with him, his gun barrels resting dangerously in the crook of his arm and pointing towards his neighbour. " I see you are using No. so-and-so shot " he has said in a voice he has found difficult to control. When the offender shows surprise either at a good guess, or at this strange announcement, it has been pointed out to him that his neighbour could see down the barrels of his gun.

Those who call themselves sportsmen and who behave in this manner, or who handle a gun and shoot without care and attention for the safety of others, not only earn for themselves an unenviable reputation, but seldom receive invitations to shoot, and for this they have only themselves to blame. Whether shooting grouse on the open moors, pheasants, partridges and hares among the woods and fields, wildfowl along the shore, or pigeon, rabbits, vermin or clays—whatever you are shooting, wherever you are shooting, whenever you find yourself in charge of gun or rifle, remember that you are handling a dangerous lethal weapon and that one act of carelessness, one single risk taken may well bring about a serious or fatal accident—an accident that may haunt you all your days, or darken for you a future of prospective good sport and companionship.

CHAPTER THREE

Guns and Cartridges

*Home Truths—Choosing a Gun—Cartridges and Loads
—Shot Sizes—Pattern and Penetration—Single Barrel
Guns.*

RIGHTLY or wrongly, I am confining this chapter on
guns and cartridges to the few really necessary elementary facts that a young shooter should know about his weapon
and ammunition. The subject of guns and cartridges is a
wellnigh inexhaustible one. Many young sportsmen may
be interested in the technical side of ballistics ; they may
have keen and enquiring minds which want to know all
about the mechanism of guns and the loads of cartridges.
To them I would say go to a sympathetic gunmaker and
persuade him to explain to you in brief the process of how
guns are made and of the different types manufactured for
specified purposes, and of how cartridges are loaded for
specific objects. You will learn more in half an hour of
practical demonstration than I should be able to explain to
you in the course of several chapters.

Many sportsmen show a great interest in ballistics, trying
out this cartridge and that cartridge, this load and that load.
Some seem never satisfied unless they are trying something
new, presumably to improve their shooting, which, in truth,
is probably at fault for some quite different reason. Others,
with money to spend, periodically have new guns built to
suit their fancy. The subject of guns and cartridges can be,

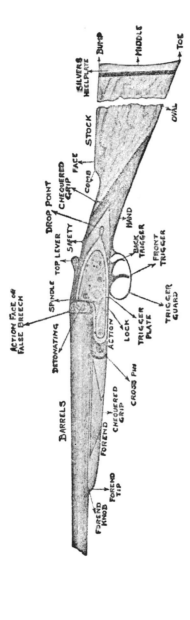

A 12-BORE HAMMERLESS EJECTOR SHOT-GUN

(From "The Shot-Gun" by T. D. S. Purdey and Capt. J. A. Purdey)

as I have said, a most interesting and intricate study and one which may be said almost to be a separate one from that which concerns the shooting field proper. At the same time, I should be the last man to discourage an interest in guns and ballistics ; what I intend to convey by the foregoing remarks is that the young shot need not concern himself unduly with complicated facts, but may become an efficient sportsman and shot at very little cost to himself. What he cares to spend on guns and equipment depends thereafter on the depth of his purse, while there are many ways open to him to follow the intricacies of advanced ballistics, should he so desire. A friend who is an expert on guns and ammunition, or a gunmaker, can quickly explain to him the particular problems that exercise his mind.

The average budding sportsman, however, should not allow himself to become puzzled and confused by talk concerning the mechanism of guns and involved conversation about loads. There is an elementary basis to all these matters and from it he can, in due course, become gradually conversant with facts that will interest him. And it is this elementary basis to which I shall confine myself—to those simple facts and figures that even the youngest shooter can assimilate. Should he, on the other hand, desire to make an exhaustive study of guns and ballistics, or should he require a quick answer to the more ordinary questions which sometimes crop up in the gunroom, then I would recommend him to read *The Modern Shotgun* (three vols.), or a little book, *In the Gunroom,* by the same author—Major Gerald Burrard, D.S.O.

To begin with, let us take the selection of a gun. Owing to age and stature, from the age of from ten to eighteen full-weight weapons are generally unsuitable. In any case, with changing figure and physical development, a gun would have to be altered in the stock—certainly by the time that the age of eighteen had been reached. The price of a weapon would obviously be moderate—say upwards of £100, although suitable second-hand guns may be procured at a lesser figure. It is unnecessary to invest in a high-class gun at this stage, but that is not to say that a shooter of the right sort would neglect his weapon, whatever the price. I shall have something to say about the care and cleaning of guns a little later.

Shotgun calibres are designated by the number of spherical balls of pure lead which go to the pound, each ball having the same diameter as the bore. The diameter of an 8-bore, therefore, is the same as that of a 2 oz. ball of lead ; of a 12-bore as that of a 1⅓ oz. ball, and so on.

The actual choice of bore, be it a light 12-bore or a smaller bore, is largely a question of personal preference. Some young sportsmen seem to prefer the narrower aiming plane of a smaller bore, but I contend, at the dire risk of arousing the wrath of small-bore enthusiasts (and their number is legion), that it is wise to get used to a 12-bore from the start. The ·410, it is true, cannot be beaten for a boy of tender years, but, once serious shooting at game is commenced, then the light 12-bore seems to me to be the obvious choice. I do not say that a medium step may not be taken ; that a boy who has been enjoying his earliest days with a ·410 should not graduate to a 12-bore after a season or two with a 20-bore. The modern 20-bore, with suitable loads, has a range almost equal to the larger gun ; at the same time the two governing factors connected with successful performances in the shooting field are even distribution of pattern and good penetration. Special and well-bored small bores, with specific loads in their cartridges, can be made to give a performance almost equal to that of 12-bores.

The normal chamber length in all bores is 2½ inches. The 2 in. chambered 12-bore is a comparatively recent invention. As its charge is small in relation to the diameter of the bore, a short column of shots results, which means low pressure and minimum pellet disturbance. Hence good results. If a 20-bore is chosen, its normal load is ¾ oz. of shot. The normal load of the 2 in. case 12-bore is ⅞ oz. of shot. These are quite effective up to 35 yds., which is all that is necessary.

The 2 in. case 12-bore for instance, combines power and lightness, being actually rather lighter than a 20-bore while firing a slightly heavier load. Whatever gun is finally chosen, it should not weigh more than 5¾ lb. to 6 lb. This should be " measured " at a shooting school, or by a gunmaker, to see that the stock fits well—a very important factor. If for some reason this cannot be arranged, then it must be remembered that the stock should be rather too short than too long, for if it is too long it may catch in coming up to the shoulder, or the shooter may fail to get his finger properly round the front trigger which fires the right-hand barrel.

British made guns, proofed to withstand the loads marked on the flats of their barrels are, of course, the best. Highly priced guns are built for wear. Such are necessary for sportsmen who fire thousands of shots a season, but for the Young Idea, who will probably fire no more than a hundred or two shots in a year, a hammerless non-ejector is good enough. Buy the best gun you can afford ; see that the stock fits ; try out the effects of pattern on a white-washed target of iron, or on a large square sheet of stiff paper ; show the result of such shooting to a friend with some experience of elementary ballistics, and you cannot go far wrong.

There are two main types of hammerless gun actions, one being the side lock and the other the Anson and Deeley, often referred to as the box lock. The relative merits of the two types is a subject of much discussion and argument. The side lock is an action which is fitted to the majority of " best guns," the working parts of which are assembled together on separate plates which are let into the sides of the stock. Not only does this method of construction lend itself to a design of mechanism which makes fine adjustment possible, but it also permits graceful and pleasing lines and gives full scope to the engraver's art.

The Anson-and-Deeley action has fewer working parts than a side-lock action and the mechanism is much less complicated as a result. The working parts of this action are set up as a single unit and not assembled on two separate plates as is the side lock. It is for this reason that a box lock is cheaper to produce than a side lock and is consequently used on the average cheap and medium priced gun. Briefly, then, if you are buying an expensive gun, you should decide on a side lock, but if your purse is limited, then choose a box lock as, whilst a really good quality side lock is to be preferred to a similar quality box lock, there can be no doubt that a good box lock is a better " investment " than a cheap side lock. Just as, generally speaking, a motorist prefers a good six-cylinder engine to a four-cylinder one, so would he prefer a good " four " to a poor " six."

If the young shooter wishes to delve more deeply into this intriguing subject, I would refer him to the books I have mentioned earlier in this chapter by Major G. Burrard.

The boring of a gun is most important. If it is required for driven game, both barrels could be bored improved cylinders. True cylinder barrels allow of a wide spread of shot ; improved cylinder infers that this spread is slightly restricted, so that a closer pattern is made over the same range. Half-choke boring still further tightens up the pattern, while full-choke barrels will place a comparatively close pattern on a target at forty yards.

When a gun is to be tested, it is fired at a whitewashed iron plate at 40 yds., when a circle of 30 in. in diameter is drawn round the thickest part of the pellet marks. The spread of these marks is called the pattern. An improved cylinder (a very slight choke) should put 50 per cent, a half choke 60 per cent and a full choke 70 per cent of the pellets of the charge into such a circle. Even distribution of

27

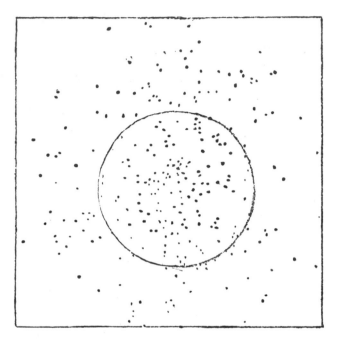

12-BORE, 2½-IN. CASE, IMPROVED CYLINDER, AT 40 YARDS: 33
GRAINS SMOKELESS DIAMOND AND 1¹⁄₁₆ OZ. OF NO. 6 SHOT.

pellets is necessary, or game may escape through gaps in the pattern.

Choke is a constriction of from 3- to 40-thousandths of an inch towards the muzzle end of the barrel, varying in shape and length according to the patterns to be obtained. There are three main degrees of choke—improved cylinder (·003/·005 in. constriction), half choke (·015/·020 in.) and full choke (·035/·040 in.).

Before choke boring was introduced, extra range was gained by the use of shot concentrators, of which the Eley " wire " cartridge was one of the best. These devices held the shot together for a time after leaving the barrel, but choke boring and improved loading technique with heavy loads have made them redundant.

The standard shot load for a 12-bore is $1\frac{1}{16}$ oz. To give some idea of the range and killing powers of this load, here is a table of pellets to be found in a 30 in. circle at varying ranges and using Nos. 4, 5, 6 and 7 shot :

CONDITIONS. Range in yards	30	35	40	45	50	55	60
No. 4 Shot (181 pellets).							
True cyl.	109	89	72	60	47	38	31
Impvd. Cyl.	130	110	91	76	60	49	40
Half Choke	150	129	109	91	72	58	47
Full Choke.	181	152	127	107	89	72	58
No. 5 Shot (234 pellets).							
True Cyl.	140	115	94	77	61	49	40
Impvd. Cyl.	168	143	117	97	77	63	51
Half Choke	194	166	140	117	94	75	61
Full Choke.	234	196	164	138	115	94	75
No. 6 Shot (287 pellets).							
True Cyl.	172	141	115	95	75	60	49
Impvd. Cyl.	207	175	144	120	95	77	63
Half Choke	238	204	172	144	115	92	75
Full Choke.	287	241	201	169	141	115	92
No. 7 Shot (361 pellets).							
True Cyl.	217	177	144	119	94	76	61
Impvd. Cyl.	260	220	181	151	119	97	79
Half Choke	299	256	217	181	144	115	94
Full Choke.	361	303	253	213	177	144	115

Regarding powders (which, as even the youngest of us interested in guns knows, drive the shot up the gun barrels on exploding), 33-grain bulk powders, such as Smokeless

Diamond E. C., etc., were most popular for ordinary use.*
They are called " bulk " because they take up the same space
in the cartridge as the old 3 dram measure of black powder—
a powder which, when fired, gave out a terrific report, with
flame and smoke belching from the gun.

Much controversy rages round the question of the best
size of shot to use for different occasions. Those used for
game shooting, as distinct from wildfowling, are Nos. 5
(there is also $5\frac{1}{2}$), 6 and 7. There are 220 No. 5's to an ounce,
or 234 to a standard $1\frac{1}{16}$ load. 270 No. 6's to an ounce, or
287 to a $1\frac{1}{16}$ load ; 340 No. 7's to an ounce, or 361 to a
$1\frac{1}{16}$ load. Roughly speaking, Nos. 5 and 6 shot are used for
shooting game-birds, hares and rabbits, and pigeon and other
" tough " birds at reasonable ranges, while No. 7 shot,
although used for game by some sportsmen (in my estimation
wrongly so), is usually confined to snipe shooting, or for
killing rabbits at short ranges.

For wildfowling, for long-distance shooting at heavy
birds such as geese, there are a variety of shot sizes from
SSG (15 pellets to the ounce, or 16 to $1\frac{1}{16}$ oz.) to No. 4 (170
to the ounce, or 181 to $1\frac{1}{16}$ oz.).

Cartridge cases usually have $\frac{5}{8}$ in. or $\frac{5}{16}$ in. brass heads,
but deeper brass heads or all-metal cases can be procured at
a higher price, brass cases and waterproofed cases being used
mainly for wildfowling. But for ordinary game shooting
waterproof best quality cases are by no means essential.

One of the more recent innovations of note in the ammunition world is that of the crimped cartridge. This means
a cartridge with no overshot wad. For years there had been
a theory that this was to some degree responsible for occasional
" cartwheel " or scattered pellets, by interfering with the
flight of the pellets after emerging from the barrel. Now

* Today we are reduced to two "basic" powders, Nos. 60 and 62
manufactured by Messrs. I.C.I.

30

there are on the market several top-wadless cartridges such as the all-metal, the waxed waterproof paper and a paper-covered metal cartridge. Exhaustive target tests have proved that this system does give very fine even patterns averaging about 5 per cent more pellets in the 30 in. circle at 40 yards. Less powder may be used and standard penetration maintained. The end of the case is merely crimped over the top of the shot charge.

Velocity (*i.e.* the speed of pellets over a given distance) is tested over 20 yards range. The standard is about 1070 ft. per second. All usual shot sizes have plenty of penetration. Usually, penetration outlasts density of pattern.

As to that bogey known as recoil, this should not be noticed by any normal boy, although a fully loaded 12-bore, if not held firmly into the shoulder, may kick or jar unpleasantly. Also if a large number of shots is fired, a certain amount of bruising may result, but with a gun properly held, recoil should be hardly noticed.

Nor need I say much concerning the " advantage " of a single barrel gun. Many boys have served their apprenticeship with such weapons, but my advice is, whether the young shot commences his shooting life with a ·410 or a light 12-bore, avoid if possible using a single barrel, for with it may develop faults that later may be difficult to eradicate, such as that of looking along the barrel as though it were a rifle and acquiring the habit of shutting one eye and " poking " or stopping the necessary swing.

The ideal game gun, for all-round shooting, has its right barrel improved cylinder ; its left barrel half or three-quarter choke. Other borings are a matter of taste. A gun with true cylinder barrels is rather too much of a scatter gun, its open pattern likely to " spray " a departing covey, wounding much game. A first-class shot, able to place his charge of shot exactly where he wants it to go, might prefer his barrels being half, three-quarters or even full choke. Thus the pattern

31

would be preserved over a long range, but it would have to be accurately applied to account for the game shot at. Between extreme borings are half, medium and improved— a matter for choice and taste dictated by experience in the shooting field or by the target.

Barrel length is largely a matter of preference. There is no practical difference in ballistics between the 25 in. barrel and the 30 in.

Large-bore guns, from the 3 in. magnum 12-bore to the heaviest of shoulder weapons, need not concern the young shot. Later, when he has reached a higher standard of physical development, he will be able to further his education concerning guns beyond the confines of this book. In the meantime the range of bores that come within his purview are the ·410, the 28-bore (rarely used nowadays), the 20-bore, the 16-bore and the light 12-bore.

The cleaning of guns is a process that must not only be understood by the sportsman, but diligently practised. I would emphasise the fact that no good sportsman should ever leave his gun uncleaned with the intention of attending to it later, or to-morrow. However excellent may be the composition of modern powders, neglected barrels will suffer. The effect of burnt powder and a damp atmosphere will cause pitting in the barrels, and deposit and rust, forming in these, will surely play havoc even where the best material is concerned. The true sportsman on returning from shooting attends first of all to his dogs (and ferrets), then to his gun. When the dogs and ferrets have been kennelled and hutched and fed, then the essential business of drying and cleaning the gun must be accomplished, even before the personal comforts of the shooter himself are considered. Having thoroughly dried the external surface of the weapon, giving every care to the crevices and available mechanised parts, wipe out the interior of the barrels with tow or flannel patches. Now insert some cleaning oil and use a bristle brush. Wipe dry and oil with Rangoon or vaseline (if temporarily to be put aside) on wool mop. Keep the gun in a case in a dry room. Cleaning rods, cases and snap-caps may be procured from any gunmaker. The latter are " dummy " cartridges, specially made with a spring plunger substituted for the usual primer. This enables the gun to be " fired " without risk of breaking the firing-pins or injuring other working parts. Snap-caps are very useful for practice, etc.

No hammer gun should be left for any length of time with the hammers cocked but, despite ancient theories to the contrary, nothing is gained by " easing springs " with a hammerless gun. This practice can, indeed, be actively harmful.

CHAPTER FOUR

How to Shoot

Confidence—Swing and Footwork—Eyesight—General Stance—Variety of Shots.

THE greatest aid to successful shooting is Confidence with a capital C. Without confidence in oneself, in one's gun and in one's cartridges, it is impossible to shoot well. I know otherwise consistently good shots who, for one reason or another (perhaps illness, tiredness, worry or because their weapon or cartridges are not what they habitually use) have " muffed " a day's sport simply because they have not been " up to scratch," and accordingly the usual confidence with which they performed in the field was lacking. Not that the matter of a strange gun or borrowed cartridges should have a bad effect on a good all-round shot ; but there are men, specialists at certain types of shooting, or those who are highly strung, that can be fairly easily put off their shooting, even though they are known to be good shots under normal conditions.

Strange though it may seem, there appear to be some sportsmen who have a curious effect on certain people who shoot in their company. I, myself, have a friend who often shoots with me and in whose presence I all too often shoot below my average form. I cannot explain why this should be, for I am used to shooting in the company of every type of sportsman and am by no means of a nervous disposition ; nor do I suffer from " stage fright." Nevertheless, it is obvious that my nerves are in some way disturbed in his company, and realising this, I apparently suffer from slight lack of confidence.

34

There have been times, too, when I have been forced to use a brand of cartridge in which I have not had full confidence, although others are performing well with them. In a chapter on snipe shooting I have explained how the common belief that snipe are one of the most difficult birds to shoot is apt to undermine the confidence of the young shot, whereas, if this belief had not been on his mind, he might find himself shooting comparatively well.

The moral of all this is, of course, to force confidence in yourself upon yourself and try hard not to give way to fancies that have no foundation in fact. In watching game approach, train yourself to remain cool and undisturbed until the moment comes to shoot. If excitement or doubt gets the better of you, you will find yourself missing again and again.

The next most important factors towards becoming a proficient shot are what is known as " swing " and footwork. It is, of course, necessary to shoot ahead of moving objects and the lead or allowance given must depend on the speed and angle of those objects. It is obvious that no rule of thumb can be laid down in this respect, for only practice and experience teaches the beginner how far ahead of his game he must shoot in order that the charge of shot will reach its objective. However, the general principle of successful shooting is the swinging of the gun with and in front of the bird, and to keep swinging it until after the trigger is pressed. Do not worry so much about allowances, but keep the gun moving. The question of lead will then gradually unfold itself, and practice at " clays " thrown from a trap, or from a hand-flinger, or deliberate practice for experimental purposes at pigeon will be of considerable help in this respect.

Common advice given to beginners is this : " Do not squint down the barrel of your gun, but keep both eyes open and be just conscious of the barrels." While this advice is sound in a general sense, it should be remembered that eyesight differs considerably in the individual, and while it may be of advantage for one sportsman to keep both eyes open, another will be handicapped in this respect and will shoot far better with one eye closed, or half-closed. In a visit to the shooting school, the coach will immediately tell you which is your master eye and indicate the best method to be adopted with the eyes when shooting. What is known as a try-gun will be handed to the pupil, this being a gun which can be adjusted in many forms. The proper length of stock will be assured, and if a certain amount of cast-off in this is necessary it will be allowed for in due course. On a recent visit to a shooting school, to watch some young shooters being coached, it suddenly struck me that I was unaware exactly what I did with my own eyes when shooting. I was quickly enlightened when the coach put me through a simple test, and I discovered that I shot with the right eye fully open and the left three-quarters closed. The conclusion to be drawn from the matter of eyesight is this : If you find you can shoot better with one eye partly, or nearly, closed, then continue to shoot in this manner, despite haphazard advice to the contrary. If, however, you find you are shooting badly and it is suggested that you try to shoot with both eyes open, then experiment along these lines, unless you can go to a coach for expert advice. When actually shooting at game, the eyes must be kept on the bird rather than on the gun. Never dwell on aim, but fire as soon as possible after the gun comes into the shoulder. The whole body must be kept moving with the bird and not just the arms. If you do not swing as you should do and follow through, you will take to the fault of " poking," which means that you will make a rapid calculation concerning the lead necessary and will poke up the gun on to an imaginary spot ahead of the bird and fire. This is both an ugly and unsatisfactory method of shooting and one which must be discouraged at all costs in the young shot.

While waiting for expected game, the most comfortable

position in which to hold the gun is to keep the weapon across the lower part of the body, with muzzle downwards and stock under the right forearm. This is the " ready " position. The left foot should be slightly forward, and the weapon be gripped firmly, but not tightly. The first finger should be along the trigger guard, but never on the trigger until the time comes to shoot. The general stance must be a firm one, but the body must be kept supple, with weight balanced forward on the toes.

Footwork is said to be the secret of good shooting, but I never have agreed with those who give it undue importance, impressing on the beginner that the feet must be just so for this and that particular type of shot. It is one thing to tell the young shooter that, for a shot going away to the right, he must move his feet well round, pivoting on the left foot, or that for very high overhead shots he must get his right foot well back to take the weight of his body. Such instructions are strictly correct and will be followed by good results. But if the tyro is threading the junipers on the steep hillside, climbing the almost precipitous boulder-strewn ride of a covert, or walking over quaky marsh or bog, how is he to remember and follow such conventional instructions when a woodcock or snipe springs up, or a covey bursts from cover ? I would say to the young shooter, then, pay all due importance to footwork, realising that the swing of the gun, and the swing of the body depend to a great extent on footwork, but be prepared and train yourself to shoot under all manner of circumstances, almost with one leg in the air ! Above all, be natural in all you do, for, on the very rough shoot and in wild country, instructions on how to shoot contained in the text-books will avail you little, while being worthy of study under more comfortable conditions.

There are, of course, instructions to be studied, relating to lead, etc., which unless they are followed, practised and become part and parcel of the instinct of successful gun performance only poor results will be obtained. For instance, it is obvious that one must swing well ahead of crossing shots, particularly if the bird is travelling at speed. Just how far can be gauged only through experience, by the shooter himself. Practise at clays and live pigeon should be a great aid to him, for on them he can experiment in a manner that it would be impossible to follow in the shooting field proper. Always, where possible, take birds coming at you, for reasons which I have explained elsewhere. Blot out such game as the gun comes up and press the trigger, and do not be disheartened if this process of " aim " takes a bit of getting used to, for difficulty will at first be found in dealing adequately with oncoming game, although, again, a lesson on clays thrown towards you as you stand well back in a pit will go far to show you the exact timing for such shots. There are, of course, a whole variety of shots to be met with, particularly when wildfowling, and certain of them, such as curling, twisting or descending birds may need months of experience before the necessary judgment and skill to deal with them become developed.

CLAY-PIGEON THROWER

A. Pivot of two jaws.
B. Pivot of jaws and handle.

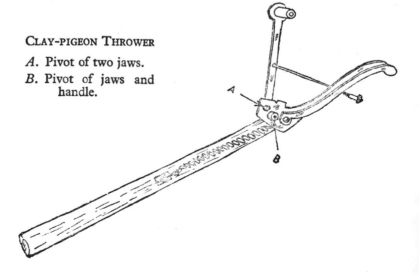

CHAPTER FIVE

Behaviour in the Shooting Field

General Manners—When Silence is Golden—" Game can Hear and Game can See "—Long Shots—When and What to Shoot—" Poaching "—Marking down Birds.

WHEN invited to join a shooting party, whether game is to be shot, or merely rabbits and pigeon, it is only a matter of common courtesy (if the invitation arrives by post, or, in one's absence from home, by 'phone) to let your prospective host know as quickly as possible if you will be able to accept his invitation, or must, for some reason, decline with thanks. To send word to him on the morning of the shoot that you cannot join him, or to arrive without having let him know that you have accepted his invitation, is not only discourteous, but may cause him uncertainty as to the number of guns to be present, or leave him to discover, at the last moment, that he is a gun short.

If you have the opportunity of getting in touch with him, find out approximately how many cartridges you may require, and whether he would like you to bring a dog—always providing your dog is steady to shot and not one of those only half-trained animals on which you cannot depend and which is as likely as not to run in and spoil the sport of fellow-guns. Make sure of the place where you are meeting, and having ascertained this and the time you are expected, leave yourself ample time on the morning in question to arrive punctually. A sportsman who earns the reputation of turning up late, and so keeping the party waiting, is not popular, and your host will not be pleased at the delay, even though his good manners may prevent him from showing his true feelings. Having arrived at the meeting-place, listen carefully to the plans for the day, but do not seek to criticise them, unless you are asked to do so. Even if you know the ground well and consider that the general plan of campaign could be improved upon, remember that you are a guest and that, as such, you must fall in with your host's decision.

Let us suppose that plans for the day include game-shooting. Either fields are to be walked-up, or birds to be driven over butts, or stands. On approaching the line of country where the first operations are to take place, try, as far as is possible, to keep out of sight of open ground. Above all else stop talking loudly and try, instead, to take in the lie of the ground and the possibilities of the first " beat." Remember, " Game can hear and game can see." Game, moreover, is blessed (or should I write cursed ?) with an instinctive sense of foreboding on seeing a party of men advancing. Pheasants and partridges, wary of what is afoot, may run into cover, or take wing, if their suspicions are unduly aroused. Accordingly, a party of guns, walking from the meeting-place to the scene of the first drive, or to where operations are to start, should do so, when in the vicinity of the ground to be shot over, as noiselessly as possible, taking advantage of sunken roads, hedges, walls, or banks to keep out of sight.

The sportsman, too, should give his thoughts, while walking from one stand to another, to the surrounding country, whether he is well acquainted with it or not. If he is on strange ground, then he should try to " take in " the lie of fields and fences ; if he knows the land well, then his object should be to keep a look-out for coveys and other game. Keen observation must always be the keynote of the successful sportsman ; without it, the sport of the day loses much of its pleasure, for environment and the activity of

wild life form the background against which clever performance with the gun takes place, and without that colourful
" scenery " even perfect shooting fails to give real satisfaction.

And to a great extent the success of a shoot (except,
perhaps, a shoot where hundreds of hand-reared pheasants
are driven over the guns) depends on the individual attention
and " wakefulness " of the guns. Nothing makes a host or
keeper more annoyed than seeing, say, two guns talking
together when each should be at his stand. The sight of two
guns in conversation, strolling back to their allotted places
only when the first coveys are sighted or the first shots are
fired, not only disgusts the keen sportsman, but their movements may be observed by game coming forward, or by
game squatting within sight, with the result that it breaks
back over the heads of the beaters, or makes off to the flank.
Whether you are waiting to walk-up, or are at a stand, reduce
all movement to a minimum, stop talking and bring all your
powers of observation to bear on your surroundings.

That flock of pigeon flying against the horizon, that
stand of plover in the centre of the field, those rooks floating
about the bunch of trees in the elm hedge may have a lesson
for the observant sportsman. The pigeon flying up from their
feeding may mean that the beaters have reached their farthest
point and are about to advance. The plover standing heads
to wind will give you some idea of the direction game will
take, particularly if you know the ground well. The rooks
may mean very little, it is true, except that the ground from
which they have risen has not recently been disturbed. But
sometimes rooks will be seen circling and cawing as they fly
low over a line of country and by their very manner the
initiated will know that a fox has been put on foot and is
making away in the direction indicated by the birds. From
the direction in which it has come lies so-and-so covert, and
one wonders how many pheasants will be found there when
it is driven through before lunch.

Again, standing quietly beside the covert, waiting for the beaters to get going, the mobbing notes of several chaffinches and a blackbird tell of a hawk or an owl among the trees. The fact is noted, and presently, as the beaters advance through the wood, a bird with a flight like the woodcock's comes forward, and though a beater shouts " woodcock," the gun realises that it is, in fact, a little owl and gives it the dose of shot it deserves. A quick eye and ear, trained to note and interpret the countless signs of Nature are great assets in the shooting field. On the other hand, those who care only for gun performance and big individual bags not only miss many opportunities, but the essence of sport is foreign to their natures. Appreciation of environment, of the colour and shape of trees, of the song and the flight of birds, of the habits and characteristics of all wild creatures, of the craft and work of agriculturists, of the clever way in which the keeper is showing his game—these things and many others form a wealth of features and details that should thrill the heart of a sportsman and mean more to him than the actual pleasure he feels at killing his game cleanly to his own satisfaction and to the envy of his fellow-guns.

Another point of behaviour in the shooting field is the knowledge of what should and what should not be shot. If game shooting, make sure that your host wants hares shot if there is any doubt about it. Likewise, towards the end of the season, ask him if hen pheasants are to be spared.

There are even times when vermin should be left to go their way in peace, though not with the sportsman's blessing ! For instance, if partridges are wild, or coveys are known to be sitting close at hand, it would be foolish to fire at a passing pigeon, or even a hawk. I doubt, myself, if I could resist the temptation of killing a stoat, but that would be the only type of vermin I would permit myself to shoot under the circumstances, and I am not sure, even then, that every one present would approve ! Again, when standing at the covert-side, waiting for pheasants to rise as the beaters advance, the jay and the magpie, the weasel and the rat should be left well alone, or a shot fired just as pheasants are about to break out may well send many scurrying back into cover, or put others on wing which will turn back, on rising, to fly over the beaters' heads.

When walking to and from your butt or stand, do not be tempted to fire at a rising pheasant or covey. You may add one more head of game to the bag, but the resultant disturbance may equally well detract from the final bag by disturbing game on the ground over which you are about to shoot.

The question of taking long shots is another which commands attention. The sportsman who seems to have no idea of judging distances, or of the limited capabilities of a shotgun, is a real menace to a shoot, for not only in blazing away at birds that should be left unshot at does he wound a great many (probably pricking the ovaries of hen birds and so destroying their ability to breed), but unduly disturbs game and sends that at which he shoots winging for, or into, the next parish ! Let it be remembered that a covey rising at, say, thirty yards, is probably well over the forty-yard mark by the time the trigger is pressed, and accordingly beyond reasonable killing distance. Far better curb your anxiety to assist in filling the bag than to arouse the wrath and perhaps even the contempt of your host and other members of the party and shoot only at birds that will be well within the forty-yard limit by the time the shots reach them.

" What goes up must come down," but it is to the advantage of the shooter that game that rises, descends within the boundaries of the shoot. Indeed, if there is the slightest likelihood of missing birds that are obviously making for a nice bit of holding cover within the boundary, fire should be withheld, and the shooter stand still to mark and memorise the exact spot where the game lands.

43

To the shooting man, poaching can mean one of two things. It can refer to the practices of the poaching fraternity, or to the gun who shoots game that is nearer to, or obviously " belongs " to a fellow-gun. If, for example, a bird is approaching a stand and is nearer to that stand than any other, it should be left for the gun occupying that stand to kill it. If another gun fires at it, he is said to be " poaching." Or if a bird, a hare, or a rabbit gets up in front of a walking gun and another shoots it, he is " poaching," a form of shooting-field crime that will not be tolerated if it is often repeated. It is bad sportsmanship (if such a paradox exists), and he who acquires " a name " as an habitual " poacher " is not to be envied. On the other hand, if a sportsman misses his game and another kills it for him, then the latter is said to have " wiped the eye " of the former and much good-natured chaff will ensue at the expense of the shooter who missed.

A " jealous " shot is, in fact, a " poacher," the only fine difference, if there is one, appearing to be that a jealous shot is usually a good shot and, although he *may* not take game that too obviously " belongs " to another, if there is even the slightest doubt, depend upon it he will not hesitate to show his prowess. A better name for him than " jealous " shot is " greedy " shot, and his lack of sportsmanship and self-control deserve the censure they usually receive.

The etiquette of the shooting field proper is strict, but it may be relaxed when friends are walking round together, or on the rough shoot where guns agree " not to wait " for each other, but to shoot between them all they can, for on many rough shoots little would be killed if one stood too much on ceremony.

The unwritten laws of the shooting field, however, including good manners, safety-first procedure and proper consideration shown to game, particularly wounded game, must remain unbroken under all circumstances. In regard to wounded and even dead game, the true sportsman is not

44

content merely to " down " it and pass on. He must make exhaustive search for it, particularly if it is known to be winged, or otherwise wounded. Should a partridge fall among roots when guns are walking in line, the line must halt for a reasonable time while the bird is sought by dogs, and if it cannot be found, and the shooter can be spared for a while after the field has been walked out, he might get his host's permission to return to the spot, *i.e.* if he has a dog.

The only exception to leaving dead and wounded game is on a shooting day when keepers and pickers-up are specially engaged to gather it. Under these circumstances, the guns should carefully mark where game falls, make a mental note of any specific spot (say, where a towered bird falls at a distance, or a bird with a pricked wing comes down) and remain at his stand until keeper or picker-up arrives. To go in search of dead and wounded game is to " foil " the ground ; scent is interfered with ; the line of the running bird broken by human scent—with the result that questing dogs are baulked in their endeavours to get quickly on the line and catch up with the game. Therefore, remain quietly at your stand until a keeper comes up, when he can be told where to set his dogs on. Tell beaters, intent on searching for wounded birds, to stand back and leave them for the dogs. Do not follow other guns who break this rule. Your host and his keepers will greatly appreciate your sound sense. If, however, you have a steady dog with you, this may be sent out as soon as the drive is finished, but not until then, even when a runner falls. Many guns are apt to waste the keeper's time by saying they think they have a bird down. Make sure that a bird definitely does come down before asking the keeper to search for it.

Fallen game can be marked by taking a line from the stand to some object in view, the exact spot on that line being mentally registered as close to a thistle, tuft of grass, or some similar identification. A towered bird is usually one hit in

45

the lungs, when the blood causing a " black-out," the bird towers upwards to a height, falling like a stone to earth, to be picked up dead. Such birds, towering at a distance, may more easily be marked by the gun stooping as low as possible and checking the fall against some object along an imaginary line between the stand and the horizon, or from the stand to a nearer landmark.

To reiterate : At all times in the shooting field, keep your eyes open and your mind on the business in hand. When walking in line, see that the barrels of your gun are pointing towards the ground or the sky and do not hold your gun in the crook of the arm, with the barrels swinging dangerously along the line of guns. Remember always the comfort of others, which comfort can have no existence in the presence of a dangerous shot, or one who carries his weapon carelessly. Keep in line, watching your left- and right-hand companion, but alert for rising game, or signs of wild life that may have a possible bearing on the day's sport. Be courteous to older guns, but do not be tempted to follow the bad example of those who are less strict about shooting-field procedure and manners than they should be. Unhappily there are to-day many sportsmen of limited experience who have not made a close study of etiquette in the field, but for one reason or another their presence is tolerated. Fall in with the plans of your host and do not criticise them with fellow-guns. You may think that game is being driven badly, or that fields are being walked-up in the wrong direction. Remember, however, that you have been invited to take part in a shooting party and it is up to you to fall in with the desires of your host, and to do your best to swell the bag without taking long shots and otherwise behaving as though you were a complete tyro.

CHAPTER SIX

The Sportsman-Naturalist

What every Sportsman should be—What and What Not to Shoot—The Amateur Keeper—Tell-tale Sounds and Signs—Tracking in Mud and Snow.

I HAVE headed this chapter " The Sportsman-Naturalist," for, to gain full enjoyment from the sport of shooting, every sportsman should be a naturalist at heart and do his best to gather more than an elementary knowledge of the creatures of the countryside, their habits and characteristics, and how these may best be utilised to the benefit of sport. Those unacquainted with the principles of sportsmanship and of its economic value seem to imagine that nothing is safe from the man with a gun ; that he sallies forth and blindly shoots at almost anything that rises or squats. Anti-sport societies make great play in this respect, and when some novice, or some black sheep (of which every fold contains a small percentage) kills, say, a bittern or a hobby falcon, they flood the local papers with the news, hoping that town-dwellers and those completely ignorant of country life will be influenced to oppose all forms of field sports.

In fact, the sportsman is the defender of wild life. He preserves our game birds from the poacher and pot-hunter who, if no check were placed upon their activities, would quickly denude the countryside of grouse, black game, pheasants, partridges and hares. Seek out any woods or coverts on a spring or summer morning where game is preserved and listen to the dawn chorus of bird voices.

Search those sanctuaries (the real bird sanctuaries of these islands) and mark well how our songsters and other small and useful birds nest and breed there. If vermin was not kept in check, if such places became the playground of the public, that glorious chorus would no longer be heard. Vermin, both furred and feathered, would make inroads among our smaller birds; they would destroy eggs and young, while continued disturbance would tend to " place a damper " on this particularly delightful feature of the countryside.

Where vermin is allowed to exist and breed at will, the song of birds becomes suppressed; for their own safety they sulk in the underwood and trees, not daring to disclose their whereabouts and that of their nests. Stoats and rats (which climb trees and bushes almost as easily as squirrels), grey squirrels, jays, magpies and other ground and winged vermin, if allowed to thrive, systematically hunt for and destroy eggs and young, not only of game-birds, but of all lesser forms of feathered species, but where the gamekeeper (professional or amateur) destroys and discourages vermin, there you will find, as I have said, the true bird sanctuaries wherein one may be almost deafened by the morning and evening choir of bird voices and where the balance of Nature is nicely kept to the benefit of all concerned.

I pity the man who shoots only for shooting's sake and does not trouble to make a study of Nature. He may call himself a sportsman, but, in doing so, he labours under false pretences. What pleasure is there, except maybe the satisfaction gained from good gun performance, of standing at the covert-side shooting at pheasants driven over a stand if one " has eyes that see not and ears that hear not " ? Pleasure there is in being a good shot and enjoying the reputation that this brings, but the sportsman will tell you that his interests lie deeper. While listening to the tap-tap of beaters' sticks, expecting every second to hear the wing-beats of a rising hen pheasant, or the raucous " cock-up, cock-up " of an old cock bird crashing upwards through the undergrowth and trees, he is by no means unaware of the minor happenings taking place about him. He finds the greatest pleasure in the scenery and the sky effects ; he appreciates the manner in which game is being shown him ; his senses are alert to the event of a woodcock, a hare, a rabbit, or any other legitimate quarry coming suddenly into view. More than this, he watches with joy the blue-tit swinging upside-down on the fir branch, the yellow-hammer perched on the highest briar of the hedgerow, the scolding wren threading the intricacies of the briar bush, the fieldfare hopping about in the meadow. Almost subconsciously he notes the wheatear flitting from stone to stone, or from clump to clump on the open downs, the woodpecker leaving the covert in dipping flight for safer quarters, the kestrel hovering lower and lower over the distant fields. All these things, and a thousand more, may attract his attention and give him a sense of pleasurable knowledge without which the real sport of the day would be less colourful, less enjoyable.

The young shot who has the run of an estate, or who has his own rough shooting and who would strive to become an amateur keeper would do well to make a study of wild life. Not only will he discover a fresh hobby and one worthy of his calling, but he will find that it will greatly assist him in his love of sport. In the following chapter I have gone fairly fully into the subject of what should and what should not be shot, in relation to game and vermin. Certainly it is up to the budding sportsman to learn to differentiate between the species of raptorial birds rare or common, for the sportsman-naturalist can find no pleasure in shooting, say, a hawk or falcon that is on the list of rare birds. Gamekeepers of old would do their best to destroy by every means in their power any bird that had talons or the beak of a hawk. As a result, the little hobby falcon became very rare indeed in many districts and rare almost everywhere as a breeding species. Buzzard, which live chiefly on ground game and smaller fry, because of their predatory characteristics and of occasional crimes of killing game-birds, were shot, trapped and poisoned wholesale. Happily, the modern gamekeeper and the modern sportsman are greatly enlightened as to what birds should and what birds should not be destroyed.

Not only is the true sportsman at least something of a naturalist, but the keeper himself makes a study of wild life along very different lines laid down by his father. He no longer destroys every large bird that does not come into the game list, but, admittedly with his first consideration the preservation of game and the producing of as much game as possible for his employer, he takes an eager interest in ornithology and, with all due deference, shows quiet amusement at the old-fashioned beliefs and practices of his forebears. And, having the young shot in his care, he studiously attempts to explain to him what should and what should not be shot, and the reasons behind his decision.

On the sideboards or mantelpieces of many ancient cottages you may still see the faded remains of kingfishers in glass cases. These were shot, probably, not for the harm they did, so much as for the reason they were brilliantly pretty birds and an asset to the decorations of a room. It would be difficult to-day to find the man who would shoot a kingfisher. His action would bring about his ears the condemnation he deserves. Likewise, you will no longer see hanging from the keeper's gibbet in the wood the bodies of owls, lest they be those of that vermin bird, the little owl. True, there are exceptions, but the modern keeper, like the modern sportsman, finds pride in the knowledge that he is able to differentiate between the species of predatory birds which harm or benefit the game preserves and can recognise those which, while they are capable of doing a certain amount of damage, are nevertheless rare specimens and therefore should be given the benefit of the doubt. Such birds as the peregrine falcon and Montague's harrier are dealt with in the next chapter, and it is birds of this kind which, being capable of a certain amount of destruction while they remain about a place should yet be treated with the respect they deserve.

The young sportsman-naturalist should strive to learn to identify the calls of the commoner birds and the meaning behind them. The mobbing " pink-pink-pink " note of the chaffinchs and the scolding of blackbirds will tell him that a hawk, an owl, or a prowling cat is the cause of the bother. The " cock-up " challenge of a pheasant repeated in alarm may well show that a fox is afoot. By night, the twittering voices of disturbed larks, or the alarm cries of plover, have often given away the presence of poachers, or of Reynard crossing the open fields. But only by first-hand experience can these signs be studied and understood, when the knowledge so gained will be applied to the work of amateur keepering.

Another useful study to undertake is that of the " calling " of wild creatures by imitating their own calls (with different inflections, or notes meaning warning, contentment, call to feed, etc.). Thus, passing wildfowl may be attracted and " called " within range. The shrill whistle of the golden plover, the " pee-wit " of the lapwing, the low " quacking " of duck, the repeated flute-like whistle of curlew, redshank and other waders can be practised and eventually used with good success.

I have often " called " crows from a considerable distance. Listening for and imitating their " crrr-crrr " of invitation, I have watched a pair of cunning old birds decoyed nearer and nearer, tree by tree, until the gun spoke. But the greatest care must be taken to get the right notes (the alarm notes would only tend to arouse their suspicions), the correct inflections or tones and the right timing between calls. Magpies and jays likewise may be induced to approach within range of an ambushed gun, and no one better than the keeper can explain and teach the Young Idea how vermin birds can thus be decoyed.

Incidentally, crows, rooks, jays and magpies can also be induced to approach the hide in which the sportsman is waiting for them by arousing their curiosity with all manner of strange noises, mostly those giving some idea of an animal in anguish. Also, a cat or a ferret, or stuffed owl has served me well in the past as a " draw " to winged vermin. Tethered in a glade of the wood, it has attracted the attention of, say, a jay, when other jays have been drawn to hop about the neighbouring trees cursing the creature that is their hereditary enemy. Even a shot or two, putting paid to one or more of their companions, has failed completely to frighten them. Their curiosity and anger aroused, they have returned to their mobbing, only realising the full danger into which they have placed themselves when several of their number have been destroyed.

Every keeper is an adept at " squeaking " for stoats and weasels. By this means he is able to draw them from the shelter of cover, or from holes into which they have disappeared. This calling sound, made by the sucking-in of air between pursed lips, aided, if necessary, by the thumb and first finger being placed against them in a perpendicular position, is a supposed imitation of the sound of a rabbit or other small animal in distress. Stoats and weasels appear to be unable to resist the temptation to investigate the noise, when, the gun standing immovable, except for the slow action of the hands as they move to lift the weapon, is able to account for yet another head of vermin.

One incident, showing the effect of this " squeaking " for stoats, will always remain in my memory. For some time a stoat and her family had been seen in the neighbourhood of the rearing-field and she had cleverly avoided all our efforts to catch her. One early morning, two of us, having foolishly left our guns at the hut where we had been mixing food for the pheasants, were carrying a haversack of feed along a cart-track towards a covert on the hillside, when we spied the stoat and six young running snake-like towards us down a shallow rut. Standing perfectly still we allowed the family to come on, when we set about them with the sticks we carried, killing all with the exception of the old stoat, which popped into a rat burrow in the bank. For some time my companion " squeaked " and " squeaked," and periodically the stoat showed her head, but every effort made on our part to hit her failed. Then, foolishly, we both decided to hurry back to the hut for our guns, and this we did, leaving the bodies of the young stoats under the sack of pheasant feed. On our return my companion again began to " squeak," while I, gun ready, prepared to shoot the stoat directly she made an appearance. But " squeaked " he never so diligently, my companion failed to " draw " the stoat and eventually we decided that she had got the better of us. Picking up the haversack, however, we were surprised to discover that the old stoat had collected and carried off the dead bodies of her offspring and had evidently pulled them down the burrow.

Now the question arises, is a stoat able to count? If not, then how did the mother stoat know that she had collected the bodies of all her family? One would imagine that further " squeaking " would have raised doubts in her mind and that her curiosity would have got the better of her. However, such was not the case, and we did not see her again that day.

The young shot, particularly if he enjoys rough shooting, should learn to differentiate between the many and various tracks of animals and birds in the mud or snow. By this means it is often possible to track stoats and rats, finally to come upon them, or the burrow which they are using, when a trap may be set, or, in the case of the former creature, it may be drawn out by " squeaking."

Tell-tale signs of vermin will be seen in the mud beside

water, in that of gateways and ditches and full notice should be taken of such tracks on every occasion, until one can read them like a book. Much evidence is thus gained concerning the presence of vermin on the shoot.

Snow, of course, allows for the best possible means of reading footprints and tracks. Here a stoat has worked up a ditch-side, crossed a fallen tree to the far bank and continued its journey. Its tracks, followed up, reveal a spot where it has rolled in the snow, either in play, or to make curious and eventually catch some bird of the hedgerow. As there is no sign of blood or feathers, the scheme evidently failed. A hundred yards farther on it is obvious that our stoat has entered a pollard willow tree, and, as there are no tracks leaving it, we must draw the conclusion that it is still there. But how to bolt it ? If the tree is hollow and rotten, perhaps the dog will be able to help us. If not, it were better to fetch one or more traps and set them at the foot of the trunk. If only we had a ferret with us !

I have often followed the tracks of hares down into the water-meadows, where they have lead to forms in the reed-tussocks. Sometimes a portion of the hare is visible ; sometimes the snow has completely hidden her. Carefully we investigate, and as we approach the tussock, up springs Puss from her snug, though damp, form and makes off, offering an easy going-away shot.

The amateur keeper should remember to take full advantage of damp places, to study the tracks left by all manner of creatures, drawing from them his own conclusions. With a quickness of eye that comes with practice, he notes these things almost at a glance and passes on, reviewing the facts in his mind and giving them the consideration they deserve.

There is no doubt about it, the keeper can be a real friend and mentor to the young sportsman, and one who can teach him more in a day's walk round than he will learn from all the text-books ever written. He will show him where game-birds nest and tell him about their habits and about the habits of their enemies. He will show him, too, the nightingale's nest in the mossy bank, the long-tailed tit's lichen-covered, feather-lined home in the thorn hedge, the snipe's nest in the water-meadows. By the very nature of his calling, the keeper becomes conversant with every phase of wild life and his powers of observation are sharpened daily as he goes his rounds. Get acquainted with such a man ; show him your keenness to learn the ways of the woods and fields, but do not seek to pit the lessons gained from books against those acquired by experience. Once an apprenticeship has been served along these lines, a foundation will have been laid upon which you may build up a storehouse of knowledge— a storehouse packed with valuable and illuminating facts, gleaned at first hand from your experience afield.

CHAPTER SEVEN

Vermin

Enemies of Game—Shooting and Trapping—What and
What Not to Kill—A Formidable List—Ground Vermin
—Winged Vermin.

IT should be realised by all who enjoy the sport of shooting,
whether they are fortunate enough to have the run of a
large estate, or merely a rough shoot, that game cannot thrive
where vermin abounds, and that the chief concern of every
sportsman should be the destruction of vermin. The term
" vermin," as applied to the game preserves, constitutes
those creatures which prey on adult game, young game, or
the eggs of game. The list of species is, indeed, a formidable
one, as I shall show. At the same time, as I explained in
the previous chapter, the sportsman, while he does everything
in his power to provide and protect game, is also a naturalist,
and because of this he will use his discretion concerning the
destruction or otherwise of certain species of vermin.

To assist him to differentiate between the really harmful
kinds of vermin and those which, though loosely described
as vermin because their habits are predatory, are rare, or of
a kind that deserve consideration, I have drawn up a list of
the species most likely to be met with and have briefly outlined my views and experiences of them. Of such creatures
as the pine-marten, the polecat, the wildcat and some of the
rarer hawks, falcons and owls I need not write, except to say
that, generally speaking, as they are rare, they should earn
the respect and protection of the sportsman-naturalist. And

56

I say " generally speaking " advisedly, because there are a few districts where, say, the destruction of true wildcat may be encouraged ; even so, these exceptions need not concern the young shot—they can safely be left to keepers, shepherds and professional trappers.

Some species of vermin are best dealt with by shooting, others are more easily and systematically trapped, but neither professional nor amateur keeper, going his rounds, should neglect to carry either a 12-bore or smaller bore gun with him, or he may lose the opportunity of dealing with some head of vermin the destruction of which he has sought for days, perhaps weeks, past. And such opportunities always seem to come when the gun has been left at home, or at a distance, a fact that is all too readily recognised by experienced keepers.

Stoats.—The stoat deserves no mercy and should be shot and trapped on every available occasion. Tunnel traps, set in suitable hedgerows, or along the banks of brooks and springs, take their toll. When a stoat has been seen to disappear into a burrow, or the run of a mole, if it cannot be " squeaked " out and shot, traps should be set for it. Particularly is this the case when it is hunting with a family —a family which may number upwards to five or six and are usually born in April or May. If the old stoat is killed first, it will not be long before the youngsters will show themselves, when they may be shot, or trapped to her body. Likewise, if a young stoat is killed, traps should be brought into action, when every member of the family can be caught, if due caution, care and woodcraft are observed. But an old bitch stoat is cunning and if her suspicions are roused, she will lead away her family to fresh quarters, when it may be days before you come across them again.

The stoat is fond of fish as well as flesh, and fish-baits used are often successful and certainly worth trying.

When a stoat is in " full cry " after a rabbit, hunting that semi-mesmerised creature, leaping on and off its back and allowing it to get some distance before again taking up the line, it is in a state of bloodthirsty ecstasy and will fail to notice one, if one stands still, or even approaches steadily, making no sudden movements. Stoats are agile creatures and will climb trees and bushes like lightning, lying up in a fork, or along a branch so still that it is difficult to locate them. When trapped, or cornered, they emit a vile smell, the objectional odour coming from their scent-glands. In northern counties the fur in winter becomes pure white, only the tip of the tail remaining its natural colour—black. Incidentally, the tail of the weasel is but half the length of that of the stoat and does not have a tuft of black hair at the end as does the tail of the latter—a simple feature of identification often overlooked by the rustic.

The only good stoat is a dead stoat, for this creature not only makes inroads among game, but, as is the case with most species of vermin, furred and feathered, is an inveterate egg-stealer and destroyer of nestlings whether they be of game or of smaller fry.

Weasels.—There are some people who will tell you in defence of the weasel that it kills countless rats and mice and is therefore deserving of mercy. It is true that weasels do destroy countless small rats and mice, but they also prey ruthlessly on the young of game- and song-birds and in their ferocity will even attack full-grown partridges and well-grown poultry. Indeed, there can be few farmers and poultry farmers who have not suffered from the depredation of both stoat and weasel, and who make every effort to kill them when their presence becomes known.

On the pheasant rearing field the weasel is an even greater pest than the stoat. Being considerably smaller (although I have killed weasels almost the size of stoats, and weasels of the " mouser " kind which are even smaller than a half-grown stoat) they are able better to use the runs of moles,

58

and by doing so can stalk and snatch pheasant chick after pheasant chick, pulling them underground and out of sight before the crime is discovered and the alarm raised. Even when a rearing field has been heavily rolled, to destroy the runs of moles, weasels seem adept at finding those still usable, and we have at times been nearly off our heads to discover how it is that broods are becoming smaller and young vanishing from sight. At last, however, a weasel is seen to be attacking a chick and every effort is made to catch it under difficult circumstances. Fortunately, tunnel traps take heavy toll of weasels, but there are still plenty left to carry on the good work of which they are undoubtedly capable when birds are no longer young and can take care of themselves.

Rats.—It is hardly necessary for me to say that the prolific rat should be destroyed in every way possible. It should be shot, gassed, ferreted, trapped and snared at that time of the year when it inhabits the banks and hedgerows of harvest fields, or the coverts where pheasants are fed. Later, when the harvest is carted, and it takes to the stacks and barns, it will be more difficult to account for in numbers until the corn is threshed. Then the young shot should forget his gun for the time being, and do his best to kill every rat he can by running small-mesh wire-netting round any stack being threshed so that no rat may escape. Good sport can be enjoyed with terriers and other dogs and excellent service rendered to agriculture and the game preserves.

I have always kept a number of ferrets specially for ratting. These are of a small variety and are never used on rabbits. Pigsties, stables, barns, granaries, etc., can be ferreted, rats being shot with a ·410, or killed by dogs.

The rat is a thirsty creature and will risk its life for water. A shower falling during dry weather will bring rats out on to the thatch of barns and stacks, where they eagerly sip the drops of rain from the straw. That is the time to wait for them with a small-bore gun or a rifle. Also of an evening they will seek out ditches and pools at which to quench their thirst, when the ambushed gunner will have the opportunity of making both a fair bag and of training himself to be of good patience and to practise the art of stalking.

The trapping and snaring of rats has been dealt with in another chapter, but every method, recognised or " home-made," should be used to destroy a creature which costs the country millions of pounds a year and is an ever-present source of nuisance on the shoot.

Hedgehogs.—There is much to be said in favour of the hedgehog, and Prickles does not lack for champions. He is, we are assured, a good gardener, killing and consuming great quantities of slugs, snails and injurious insects. This is true, but I would add that he is not the kind of gardener to trust in a bed of young green-stuff! A consumer of carrion, an inveterate egg-thief, a slayer of young birds and a more active and rapid " poacher " than he is commonly given " credit " for, his presence on the shoot is not to be encouraged. Fortunately, he is comparatively easy to trap and a dog trained to retrieve hedgehogs may be expected to make good " bags " on a spring or summer's evening at dusk after a shower has fallen, or during an early morning dew.

With a small pack of dogs I used to make quite a lot of pocket-money by collecting live hedgehogs and sending them to a famous firm for purposes of research. This had the duel benefit of adding weight to my money-box and of ridding a certain famous partridge shoot of very undesirable tenants.

Grey Squirrels.—This alien pest, rightly designated the tree-rat, is responsible for many crimes, from the destruction of the young and eggs of game- and song-birds, to the raiding of orchards and gardens. The one good thing I can say about it is that it gives the young sportsman plenty of opportunity to try out his patience and woodcraft when stalking it among the trees of woodland. Once it is aware of one's presence, it will either make a bolt for the nearest drey or nest from which it can be shot, or will dodge behind a tree-trunk or branch, or freeze into a fork, or against a bough. In early spring I have shot into dreys, thereby killing whole families. It can also be trapped to such bait as Indian corn. A good dodge to try when a grey squirrel cleverly keeps the wrong side of a bough is to take off one's coat and prop this up a few yards from one side of the tree, and then walk slowly round to the other. This gets the squirrel " all mazed up," as the saying goes, and in an attempt to be on two sides of the tree at once, it offers a good shot ! Really first-class sport can be had by walking quietly through a wood where these pests are numerous, and shooting them either with a shotgun or rifle—preferably the latter fitted with a silencer. In America the grey squirrel is eaten and also canned. A grey-squirrel pie I once tasted was certainly good—while one kept one's mind off its subject matter !

Foxes.—No sportsman would harm a sister sport. Consequently, except in Scotland and in the Fell District and where no hunting is carried out, it is a crime against sport to shoot or trap foxes.

Badgers.—That ancient Briton, Brock the badger, is by no means as scarce as a majority of people would have us believe, and particularly does this remark apply to the West Country. While it is sometimes necessary for keepers to remove a few badgers when their population becomes too great, the subject of this heading does not come under " vermin," so far as the young sportsman is concerned. Rather, he should interest himself in the ways of the badger, admiring the tenacity, the " toughness " of a creature that has survived throughout the ages, despite various forms of opposition. True, badgers will destroy the nests of game-birds, if given the opportunity, but, taking it by and large, the good that Brock does outweighs the harm. He is a great destroyer of wasp-nests and of nestling rabbits, and he also acts as " housekeeper " to foxes that use his sett in which to lie up or breed. The fox is not a clean beast in its habits, dragging all sorts of food into its den where it rots, and in due course the result may be seen in foxes with mange—a skin disease that is exceedingly contagious and may eventually prove fatal. All such putrid matter is carefully removed by badgers from their sett and if, occasionally, very occasionally, a fox cub is killed by Brock, I do not believe that against the great service he renders to an inconsiderate boarder such rare crimes should be taken into account.

His personal " household " habits are a credit to him. Coarse grass, rushes and bracken with which he forms his bed are brought out from the sett to air in the sunshine and " pits " are dug away from the mouth of the sett in which he deposits offensive waste and other matter.

Because I have the greatest regard for Brock, because his chief diet consists of mice, snakes, lizards, grubs, insects, roots and bulbs (the tit-bit which his soul loveth is a squab fallen from its nest in the rookery), because I have made a rather special study of his habits and characteristics, I have no intention of dealing with the methods by which badgers are trapped and sometimes snared, for such practices are quite out of keeping with the object of this book.

Otters.—If you want to make a pet of a wild animal, I would recommend to you the otter cub—an intelligent and interesting creature ; perhaps the most intelligent and most interesting of any of our wild animals. Like the fox, it is hunted with hounds and many pleasant days have I had enjoying hound work and watching the cunning of the wild pitted against the sharp senses of a trained pack. That the otter can be exceedingly destructive on salmon and trout rivers is an acknowledged fact, and in some districts (notably in Scotland) there is a price upon its head. To the average shooting man, however, the otter is a comparatively rare animal, seldom seen, and, when viewed, best left to go about its lawful (or unlawful) occasions.

In fen country, it is to be admitted, otters do cause havoc among young wildfowl and game, and if they are then destroyed on sight let us draw a curtain over the picture.

The otter is by nature a nomad with a strong desire for travel and adventure and for good food. It also possesses a love of playfulness and an unerring instinct for self-preservation. It is equally at home in the lush coolness of osier beds where the soft, purple flower panicles of the great reed wave gently to the sigh of warm, scented winds, and the wave-washed rocks and caves of the seashore. Its seals, or footprints (five-toed), may sometimes be followed along the river bank to its holt or lair, which is often reached by an underwater entrance. Even more so than those of the badger its habits are worth studying and I feel that any young sportsman would delight in reading Mr. Henry Williamson's *Tarka the Otter*, and by doing so would add considerably to his knowledge of a particularly fascinating creature.

Seals.—The common seal, which destroys many salmon and other fish in the estuaries of rivers and sometimes inhabits inland lakes, is often shot with a rifle, but its " close " time should be studied and local sentiment probed before an expedition is undertaken.

Cats.—A good " ratter " is worth its weight in gold, but a cat (however " golden " its past may be) that takes to poaching becomes useless about the farm and its disappearance will not be mourned—except, perhaps, by an owner who has an affection for it ! Once a cat starts to wander along the hedgerows in search of young rabbits, or gets the taste of young game-birds, it seldom returns to farmyard fare. Having discovered a brood of partridges or pheasants, it will not rest until it has accounted for all, and a poaching cat of this kind becomes an adept at seizing partridges off the nest, as I know only too well from experience. Many a good cat turned poacher has deserted, or partly deserted its comfortable home, preferring to live in rabbit burrows and even to breed

63

there and bring up its kittens in a wild state. Happily. poaching cats are not difficult to catch to baited traps, while their expeditions into the fields are nearly always taken by the same route—a fact to be noted by the preserver of game !

Be it noted, too, that foxes are very fond of cats, in the sense that they will catch and kill them when opportunity allows and I have seen more than one cat, perched in a tree at dawn, that had obviously taken refuge from a fox.

There is a gravel pit on a shoot in which I was interested and here foxes used to breed in an old badger sett. The pit also contained a number of rabbit burrows. In the spring of the year, if there were plenty of rabbits to be seen sitting out on the edge of the adjoining fields, you could be certain that foxes were breeding there, for foxes seek their prey at some distance from their earths when they have young, and seldom attack rabbits on their own doorstep, as it were. In a year when foxes did not breed there, rabbits were seldom seen, for cats from a neighbouring cluster of council houses killed off the young ones. With foxes in residence, no cat dare poach in this pit and so, curiously enough, Brer Fox became the protector (albeit indirectly) of Brer Rabbit.

Peregrine Falcons.—I think we can safely leave the moorland keeper to deal with the problem of the peregrine falcon when it pays him the doubtful compliment of raiding his moor for grouse. The handsome peregrine is a bird of the cliffs, but sometimes frequents open country, especially downland. I have watched it strike down racing pigeons, and examination of some eyries discloses the legs of countless pigeon of this kind. On several occasions I have watched it stoop at a flock of golden plover, singling out one bird and outflying it. It will also attack larger birds, such as duck and curlew and, as I write, a splendid specimen looks down at me from a glass case. This particular bird stooped at a cock pheasant as it rose over the tree-tops and struck it down

64

amid a cloud of flying feathers. I have on two occasions seen a peregrine stoop at a covey of partridges flying between beaters and guns, and strike down its prey. When peregrines visited a downland partridge shoot, as they did each year, the birds would lie like stones in the cover of the thick grass, being picked up by beaters and dogs. They were too frightened by the presence of the peregrine to move, and if we did everything in our power to remove these birds, or encourage them to go elsewhere, we could hardly be blamed. While admiring the powerful and graceful falcon, we had to remember that guns paid a high price in this syndicate shoot and that they would not be too pleased if their Saturday shoot was a failure owing to the presence of a single bird, a bird, moreover, that is not nearly so rare as many of its champions would have us believe. I would, however, far rather see a peregrine shot at continually at a distance and so driven away than see it meet a sticky end.

Montagu's Harriers and Hen Harriers.—From the point of view of game preservation, these birds, though sufficiently rare to be viewed with delight, have an even more terrifying effect upon game than the peregrine. When visiting our downlands, they confined themselves to a far smaller area than the peregrine and their method of quartering the ground and " flopping about " when sandwiched between guns and beaters completely spoiled otherwise excellent partridge drives. One morning I watched a Montagu's harrier pounce on and kill three partridges squatting at intervals along a grassy bank. Nevertheless, I would condemn the man who sought to kill a harrier.

Buzzards.—The buzzard is better known to the valleys of Devon than elsewhere, although they are occasional visitors to most parts of the country. Drifting and wheeling overhead against the blue sky, uttering plaintive mewing cries, they rise higher and higher until they become mere specks in the heavens. Rabbits and insects are their main food,

65

and although they will pounce on small game-birds and sometimes crouching adults, no sportsman would wilfully shoot or trap one.

Hobby Falcons.—I regret that another glass case on the wall of the room in which I write contains a hobby falcon. I shot it by accident, thinking it to be a sparrow-hawk. I was standing, one evening, among some young larch trees, shooting pigeon with a ·410 as they crossed a gap overhead. Suddenly a flock of fieldfares flashed past and in pursuit of them a small falcon. In a flash I raised the gun and fired, and when the dog retrieved the result I was both surprised and annoyed to find that I had killed a hobby. I have watched with pleasure these birds chasing dragon-flies over our dew-ponds, or giving a magnificent display of acrobatics in an attempt to catch larks and starlings. The little hobby, as I like to hear it affectionately called, is not rare, but it does not breed in many of the places where it once did, having been persecuted by a generation of gamekeepers who were not so enlightened concerning the species of hawks and falcons as are their descendants to-day.

Merlins.—The merlin, smallest of its group, is a bird of the northern moors, although it occasionally visits the southern counties. As the hobby of the southern woodlands preys on larks and pipits, so does this tiny falcon flash over the moors, striking terror into the hearts of the smaller bird-life of the heather. That it will attack young grouse cannot be denied, and I once witnessed one strike down a snipe at which my father had raised his gun. I cannot dispute the attitude of some keepers regarding this species, any more than I can their individual behaviour when a peregrine visits their ground. I can only say that I have never attempted to kill a merlin, and I hope that I shall have no occasion to do so.

Sparrow-hawks.—Despite what its protectors say, I fear that I can hold no brief for this bird. Small though the cock may be (as is the case with hawks and falcons), it is capable of great destruction, not only among the young of game, but among smaller birds. Its habit of hunting marks it as a dangerous enemy. Flying low, it suddenly tops a hedge or wall, taking utterly by surprise a brood, or covey, or the flock of small birds feeding a few yards from cover. Many the hen sparrow-hawk have I shot on the nest at dusk, dealing with the cock as it came to the nest next morning carrying its usual offering of a plucked bird—the best method of ridding the shoot of an undesirable couple of gangsters.

Kestrels.—Kestrels do far more good than harm, except in the breeding season of young game. Mice, insects and small birds are this bird's chief diet, and for these it is seeking as it hovers over one spot on the ground, or over a bush. I have seen it hovering (hence its name " wind-hover ") low over a small juniper bush in which a linnet was hiding, and presently watched it fall like a stone, to pluck at the bush, successfully or unsuccessfully. Some kestrels are veritable " rogues," and once they find the rearing-field will continue to raid the coops, carrying away chick after chick until a complete brood has vanished. The watchful keeper, however, will make a note of the direction from which it comes, or of the tree in which it settles before making each raid and by so doing is able to add it to his list of vermin killed. I seldom hesitate to destroy the kestrel when young game is about, but once the rearing season is past, I see no reason to kill this very useful bird, unless a " rogue " takes a too great interest in young poultry. Happily, keepers are becoming increasingly aware of its harmlessness and of its beneficial qualities.

Carrion and Hooded or Grey Crows.—Although there is a striking plumage difference between the carrion and hooded crows, their structure and habits are similar. The grey and black plumage of the " hoodie " cannot be confused with the black of the carrion, but the hearts of both are pitch black. I have no good word to say of either, and, although their cunning is proverbial, they may be shot at the nest if an ambush is manned in its vicinity and the sportsman takes into account the sharp eyesight of the enemy. An excellent idea is for two, or even three persons to approach the hide and then to walk away, leaving one member of the party therein. This dodge also applies to the nests of other predatory birds. Crows can be trapped to dead rabbits, birds, fish, or eggs, the traps being carefully concealed in the earth round the body or shells and covered with natural soil or herbage.

Jays.—The blue-winged jay is not to be tolerated about the shoot, for it is destructive to eggs and young of bird life and is a raider of garden produce, particularly rows of peas. I once removed two coops of young pheasants to a small covert, and an hour later found several dead, their skulls smashed in by a powerful beak. Lying in wait, I quickly discovered the culprits to be jays. The noisy jay (silent, albeit in the nesting season) can be " called " and shot, shot to the nest by an ambushed gunner, or trapped to egg baits. Its curiosity is often its downfall and full advantage should be taken of this weakness. Jay shoots are sometimes held, one or two guns concealing themselves along a ride while others walk through the wood as " beaters."

Magpies.—As with jays, magpies should be destroyed by trap and gun, and in a similar manner outlined in the former paragraph. The nest of the magpie has a thick lining of mud and a bower of thorns. The sitting bird may either be scared off the nest with a thrown missile and shot, or a heavy charge of shot be sent into the nest, and if this fails to settle the bird, she may be killed with a charge of smaller shot as she attempts to escape. Vermin birds have a habit of dropping downwards as they leave their nests, and sometimes of twisting and darting away among the trees. Two guns are better than one on these occasions, but a single gun should steady himself up and take his shot coolly and deliberately.

68

I prefer, myself, to wait until the bird has " straightened out " after its dive from the nest, unless, of course, a host of trees does not allow of this, when it is necessary to risk a " snap " shot.

The Red-backed Shrike or Butcher Bird.—Many readers may hold up their hands in horror that this bird should be mentioned in a chapter on vermin ! But I do not propose to suggest its destruction. I mention it only because I have known it to raid pheasant coops near its nest and kill a surprising number of chicks. I once saw one attack and kill a yellow-hammer with a broken wing that was hopping along a path in front of me. I have also seen young game-birds impaled on thorns in its larder. Accordingly, do not allow it to nest where young pheasants are being reared ; on the other hand, no sportsman would kill this pleasant and interesting bird.

Gulls.—The larger species of predatory and egg-eating gulls are a greater nuisance on the moors and marshes than elsewhere, and should be trapped and shot whenever possible. The smaller gulls innocent of malpractices are in no way harmful to game or wildfowling interests and deserve every protection. The great black-backed, the lesser black-backed and herring gulls are the definite enemies of game-birds and wildfowl, and no hesitation need be felt in destroying them.

Herons.—The heron is capable of considerable damage on good trout water, and can also be destructive to the eggs and young of waders and other immature birds it comes across in the water-meadows and marshes. There is a price on its head where trout are bred or preserved, but I do not advocate its destruction except under extreme circumstances.

Cormorants and Shags.—These birds are particularly destructive along the coast, in estuaries and inshore waters, where they lay waste to fish life. Cormorants also visit inland waters, but the smaller birds, the shags, usually confine their activities to salt water. Excellent rifle practice may be had on birds drying their outspread wings and sunning themselves on rocks and posts, and fishermen will be grateful for every bird killed.

Owls.—Under no circumstance should the barn or white owl be destroyed, for the good it does far outweighs an occasional doubtful lapse. Nor would I willingly destroy a brown, or wood owl, although the following points must be studied and steps taken to prevent damage to game. Under normal circumstances the brown owl may occasionally kill young pheasants in a dark wood, but such crimes may be overlooked. It is when " unnatural " or artificial means of rearing pheasants are resorted to that this owl causes havoc. If, for instance, a hundred or two young pheasants are put into a comparatively small covert, there is no doubt that a pair or two of owls will take advantage of circumstances to " sample " them, and, having found them good and easy to come by, will continue to kill them.

When young pheasants begin to leave their coops and roost for the first time, owls of any kind, and perhaps the barn owl in particular, will often scare or buffet them from their low perches, when for the remainder of the night the startled youngsters crouch in the undergrowth, easy prey for foxes and small ground vermin.

A pair of long-eared owls nesting in a fir covert of a few acres will play havoc with small pheasants, and one nest I found, after my suspicions had been aroused, contained the remains of over a dozen pheasant chicks. Here, then, is a delicate problem which is apt to tax the sportsman who is also a naturalist. But common-sense reasoning and action under certain circumstances may be taken without unduly disturbing a dual conscience.

The short-eared owl, or grass owl can also be destructive to young game and wildfowl in its breeding-haunts. On our southern downlands, I have watched over forty of these owls, wintering with us, circling in the air at the same time, much resembling small buzzards. I cannot say that game is much upset by their presence, but I certainly would not encourage them on a snipe marsh.

The one owl, an owl that hunts in daytime as well as by night, which should be destroyed without hesitation is that foreign introduction, the little owl. Despite the strong defence that has been put up for its protection, gamekeepers and poultry farmers are too well aware of its bad habits to show any sentiment towards it. Introduced into this country, it has thrived and increased alarmingly, and I am glad to see that the majority of County Councils have decided to erase its name from the list of protected birds. A tame specimen in my possession killed overnight a full-grown wood-pigeon that I introduced into an aviary. Not only that, but, having decapitated it, it lifted the body on to the box it inhabited five feet from the ground. In many nests of this bird which I have examined, young game-birds and poultry have been found, their brains pecked out and eaten. It is true that this owl mainly lives on small mammals, birds and beetles, and it may even use the corpses of slain birds to " breed " and attract beetles; but that fact does not conceal its true character. I have watched it waiting for young rabbits to emerge from their burrows, when it has pounced on them and carried them off—an extraordinary feat for so small a bird. It also inhabits rabbit burrows, where it preys on tiny rabbits as well as the insects it finds there. So shoot and trap this alien pest on every possible occasion, and do not believe stories of its innocence—stories invented, and well circulated by members of anti-sport societies and senti- mentalists with no practical knowledge of their subject.

A Few Useful Points.—The young of vermin birds are both greedy and noisy, and this latter fact is useful, in that it will lead you to nests that might otherwise be difficult to find amid thick foliage. Walk quietly and slowly through a covert, listening for such sounds and taking advantage of your find to " wait on " the parent birds. Their destruction must then be followed by that of the young, for no birds must be allowed to starve in the nest.

Hawks, falcons and shrikes have this rather amazing faculty in common. If, say, a cock bird is shot, the hen will somehow find a fresh mate, returning with him to the nest. And *vice versa*. How far they must go in search we can only surmise, particularly with a comparatively rare bird (in some neighbourhoods) like the shrike.

Predatory birds with young of their own must kill and kill in order to feed their family, and it is when young game and young song-birds are about that this slaughter goes on. Therefore, kill the vermin and save the birds is a motto to be remembered and followed by every young sportsman, and by so doing, he not only follows his duty to sport, but assists in making the game preserves and wildfowling grounds the true bird sanctuaries of these islands.

CHAPTER EIGHT

Rooks and Rook Shooting

*When Rooks are Vermin—Flighting and Decoying—
The Rookery in May—The Rook Defended—
Summing Up.*

IN the days when farming in the British Isles was a pros-
perous industry, tens of thousands of acres of what is
now pasture was arable land. Fields of golden corn waved
and rippled in the warm winds of early summer where now
close-cropped meadows and feeding herds greet the eye. In
those days the rook was considered everywhere as a friend
to agriculture ; in spite of the fact that it destroyed a certain
amount of grain and roots, the benefit of the attention it paid
to the land lay in its wholesale destruction of wireworms,
" leather-jackets " (larvæ of crane flies), and other pests.
The earthen chambers which conceal the " leather-jacket "
are dug out whole and infected plants and roots are torn up
by the rook's powerful beak.

It is said that " Men were deceivers ever," and though I
stoutly maintain that there is no truth in this adage, it does
apply, in a sense, to certain matters not unconnected with the
rook. In the bad old days, I have known cases where those
who were in a position to draw vermin money for the destruction of the enemies of game, received payment for the heads
of young rooks, which they declared to be the heads of crows.
Rooks, of course, did not come under the heading " vermin,"
so far as vermin money was concerned, but all too often the

sportsman or his agent were made the innocent victims of an unscrupulous trick.

The plumage of adult rooks is glossed with blue, purple, violet and green reflections, though these become less conspicuous before the moult in autumn. It is difficult, however, to find evidence of these shades on the heads of young rooks. Moreover, (and this is where the trickery succeeded) the base of the beaks of young rooks, until their first winter, are covered with black bristles and the chin is feathered, exactly resembling those features which belong to the crows, both adult and young. Thus, unless one is well up in knowledge of this kind, it is easy to mistake young rooks for crows, and I fear that, at one time, goodly sums of money changed hands under false pretences. The base of the bill and the chin of the adult rook is formed of feather-denuded rough skin, a feature that is characteristic of the bird and not formed, as is sometimes stated, by the habit of digging for food in rough ground.

Despite the good character earned by the rook in this respect, both farmers and sportsmen were fully alive to the fact that " too many cooks might spoil the broth," and for this reason every rookery was hard shot in May, from the time the first young rooks left their nests to sit out plump on the swaying boughs, to the time when the last brood made itself apparent. In this way, the number of rooks in a district was systematically controlled, as it were, and flocks of the sable bird continued to be a familiar and welcome sight about the fields. Scarecrows were erected on newly planted fields, and farm hands, armed with ancient muzzle-loaders, and an ample supply of black powder, were told off to scare the birds from planted ground, laid corn and the harvest field.

There were even recognised " rook starvers " (and there still are a few), these being men not in regular employment, but content to " live rough " on what means could be gleaned from odd jobs. For a small sum, they would place their services including a muzzle-loader, at the disposal of any farmer or orchard-owner whose crops were suffering from the attention of rooks, pigeon and other feathered thieves, and the roar that rent the air, and the cloud of smoke that rose from the scene of operations when a " bird-starver " went into action, were familiar enough. Although the farmer " found " the powder for these bird-scarring expeditions, shot was never provided, but the more artful members of the fraternity, with an inclination towards a little quiet poaching, either begged, borrowed, or stole a ration of shot, or rammed down the barrel of their weapons charges of " shot " including bits of lead, small stones and even rusty nails.

To return to our subject, the rook, modern days have seen a great change in the problem of this bird. In the first place, rookeries are seldom shot to-day with that systematic efficiency with which older sportsmen attended to the business. Shooting the rookery in May was then considered a little shooting season of its own and was carried out in a sporting manner. An eagle eye was kept on the rookery and as soon as the first young rooks were seen outside the nest they were shot as " sitters " with a rifle and, from then on, until the last brood hatched, the rifle only was used on rooks that were unable to fly. In seasons when the foliage was backward, the rifle came more than ever into its own and in other years, when leaves concealed the young rooks from those below, many nestlings developed into strong flyers and these were accounted for with shotguns, the shooters being stationed well back from the trees. Even so, it was surprising how many young rooks survived this dual attention and eventually left the rookery to roost among the trees of the fields and feed with their parents about the farms.

Many blame the Bill that caused the registration of rifles and ammunition under the Firearms Act for a decrease in the interest of rifle shooting—particularly that of rook shooting in May. Undoubtedly, such restrictions did have a detrimental affect on the sale of such rifles for sport as the ·22 and the ·300. And because of this it may be said that, taking the country through, it is almost rare nowadays to find young rooks being shot with a rifle (or perhaps, to be more accurate, I should say the bullet from a rifle) in May.

Where it is thought necessary to thin out the nestlings, either because of the damage caused by too many rooks, or with an eye to rook-pie, we now find parties of shooters meeting the problem with shotguns, killing sitters and flyers alike, but partly on account of the boredom of such tactics and partly owing to the expense, a few evenings only are devoted to " thinning out the rookeries " with the result that in far too many districts rooks are rapidly increasing and rook-eries are becoming larger and new ones making their appearance.

Now, it is obvious that if you allow the local population of rooks to increase to a great extent and, by laying down acres upon acres of grass in the place of arable land the natural food supply of these birds is rapidly decreasing, either the rook must starve or gradually change its feeding habits and vary its menu. And that is exactly what is happening and with serious results. We are told (mainly by those opposed to shooting and other field sports) that the rook is not increasing to any alarming extent in the British Isles and that its population is a shifting one. In other words, the rook may greatly increase in one district to the detriment of the farmer, while in other districts more rooks would be welcome to deal with injurious pests. Be that as it may (and I am definitely inclined to dispute the fact) the game preserves are seriously affected where rooks are far too numerous for the available food supply.

Those of us who have studied the rook problem and have had experience of the habits of rooks under various conditions realise only too well that the forced change in feeding habits are detrimental to both farmer and game preserver and, under the circumstances, rooks may be pronounced as vermin and given a place high up in the list of undesirables. For many years I was interested in a downland shoot of over 3000 acres and, at the same time, was actively engaged in the destruction of vermin on an excellent partridge shoot on the lowlands at the foot of the downs. For miles around, the adequate shooting of rookeries in May had been badly neglected, with the result that we were forced to deal with birds the natural food supply of which could not possibly meet their needs. Over a period of years we found the rooks becoming more and more carnivorous and more and more inclined to hunt fields and hedgerows, woods and banks for nests of game-birds. Their damage to crops became a growing problem and the boldness with which they raided stackyards and fowl-runs for the eggs of poultry was startling evidence that their habits were rapidly assuming those of their cousins the crows. And while the game preserver found himself faced, as usual, with destroying a few pairs of crows, the number of rooks that raided his ground became a seemingly insolvable riddle.

Let me give you one or two facts to illustrate my con-demnation of the situation. On the downland shoot, we practised the so-called Euston System of collecting partridge eggs and placing them under hens until they chipped, when the eggs would be carefully taken from the hens and placed under sitting partridges. The partridges, in the meantime, had been supplied with dummy eggs of wood, painted to resemble the genuine article. In one season alone we lost over a hundred dummy eggs, and a great many of these were discovered during the autumn and winter about the fields, to which the rooks had taken them. They had been well pecked in an endeavour to crack the " shell." Often, in the course of our rounds, we came upon a rook making off with a dummy egg, this being dropped as a shot was fired at the raider.

At the side of a small fir covert we had two open breeding-pens for pheasants, and it was found necessary to keep constant guard over these and to collect the eggs several times a day, as rooks descended into the pens and seized the eggs if no one was handy to scare them off and, of course, we could not shoot them, as the disturbance would have scared the pheasants.

Again, on the rearing-field, if a sharp eye was not kept constantly on the coops, down would come the rooks to kill the chicks, and there is no doubt, if these raids had not been checked very few of the three thousand pheasant chicks would have survived. Nor, I may add for the benefit of those not conversant with such conditions, have I inclined towards exaggeration in the foregoing statements, as the keepers concerned and those of neighbouring rearing-fields, will be only too pleased to corroborate.

In a dry spring, when herbage was backward, and what made its appearance was immediately grazed by sheep, nesting accommodation was scarce and early pheasant nests in the open were easily and eagerly discovered by rooks that quartered the open ground. Needless to say, we waged relentless war on them, showing them no more mercy than we did carrion crows ; even so, since one cannot be in a dozen places at once, their activities often became a real nightmare to us.

On lowland ground I have watched pairs and little parties of rooks hunting the banks and hedgerows for nests and broods, but, fortunately, herbage has grown into good cover by the time partridges have begun to nest, and far less damage by rooks accrues here than in open country. That rooks are carnivorous no one with any knowledge of their ways will deny. I have watched half a dozen birds descend on a leveret revealed by the cutter, or lying on plough, and tear it to pieces, and many a " stop " of young rabbits revealed by the plough have met with the same fate. I have also borne witness to the fact that, soon after daybreak, rooks will " hunt " a wood and destroy the eggs and nestlings of song birds.

ROOKS AND ROOK SHOOTING

The seriousness of the position, however, is that nestling rooks are fed on eggs and flesh, and, being brought up on this diet and later taught by their parents to hunt, they are imbued with a murderous instinct that was once almost alien to these members of the corvine tribe.

It must be admitted that I have drawn a sorry picture of the rook, but I have purposely done so in order to convince those, where rooks are far too numerous for the available food supply, that these birds must be kept in check. Where rooks are fewer and less inclined towards bad habits, it may be difficult to associate them with the black deeds I have outlined.

The solution of the rook problem is, of course, to give proper attention to the rookeries in May and, where the stock of adults is obviously too great, to deal with it much after the manner in which one deals with the pigeon plague. Rooks may be shot flighting, and even drawn to decoys, but the eye and the senses of these birds are much sharper than those of pigeon, and perhaps for that reason it may be said that the sport of coming upon terms with them is so much the greater.

In some rookeries the eggs are taken from the nests by climbers and only a small percentage allowed to hatch out. In a few cases, where large rookeries have to be dealt with, watchers are employed day and night to keep the birds from their nests when it is judged that a majority of clutches are nearly due to hatch. Thus, the eggs get chilled and the partly formed young die in the shells.

Much " capital " is made out of this May shooting of rookeries by the anti-sport societies and individuals, vide the popular Press in May. They contend that there is no sport attached to shooting harmless nestlings, while the parent birds, circling over the trees well out of range, suffer considerable mental anguish. To a certain extent the truth of these contentions cannot be peremptorily dismissed, but

79

the livelihood of mankind and the economic value to the community of field sports are factors of our civilised life which remain of major importance, and though the sportsman does everything in his power to relieve or obviate the suffering of the creatures he pursues, it is quite impossible for him, or any one else, altogether to prevent pain, both physical and mental. As I have later pointed out we kill the rat at sight, and if it is an old doe rat it is probable that her young are left to starve in the nest. If it is a litter of young rats that we destroy, no doubt the mother suffers heartache at her loss. I dread to think what would happen if a high percentage of rooks was not shot in the early stages of their existence. Probably, in defence of the national food supply, wholesale slaughter of old birds by poison and traps would be necessary. It is far better that parent birds should suffer temporary mental pain, for I have no doubt that it is merely temporary and only short-lived. Once the shooting of the rookery is over, adult rooks resume their daily habits and we hear no more cries of fear and protest from them.

To sum up, I think I have made it clear that rooks should be included on the vermin list where they prove to be numerous and therefore become pests to agriculture and to the game preserves. On the other hand, when there would seem to be sufficient local food supply for the rook population (and thanks to the Government subsidy allowed on grass and wasteland put under the plough, there is now far more arable land than there was last year) the bird should be treated with the respect it deserves, except for the shooting of the young in May.

From time immemorial, the rook has been associated with the peacefulness and contentment of rural England. It has been sentimentalised by lovers of the countryside and im-mortalised by poets. It has been blessed and cursed alter-nately by tillers of the soil. Around it have gathered legends and stories of its sagacity—some deserved, others exaggerated.

Learning how to aim

Coaching a young shot

The raucous though pleasant " music " of the rookery lends charm to the quiet atmosphere of spring and summer days, and I, for one, would dare to say that without the rook, without the sight of those morning and evening flights trailing across the sky in loose and noisy formation, a strong link with the England reflected in Gray's *Elegy* must part.

As a game preserver and one whose feet are planted deep in the soil, I have painted the subject of this chapter as black as is the plumage of the crow, but only in relation to its existence in undesirable numbers. Also, I have written in its defence. I can only hope that those who read what I have written will draw a fine balance, a good judgment and a reasonable discernment from the given facts. I am aware that much of what I have said will rouse resentment and opposition among the more impetuous but less knowledgable members of anti-sport societies. But for this I am prepared, being already well battle-scarred in the defence of my studies and contentions.

CHAPTER NINE

Trapping and Snaring

Enemies of Game—The Tunnel Trap—The Baited Trap—Illegal Traps—The Trapping and Snaring of Rabbits and Rats—Moles.

THE key to successful game preservation, whether the ground concerned is staffed by a number of keepers, or whether it is just a small rough shoot, is the destruction of vermin, and while the gun can and does do its share in this respect, the chief weapon of offence against vermin must always remain the trap. Game and vermin cannot live peacefully together, and every head of vermin killed helps towards an increase of game.

Take one or two illustrations of this. Both stoats and rats are great egg-eaters, and the stoat in particular will seize a sitting bird and feast like a lord on her flesh, afterwards taking her eggs. If the bird, a partridge, let us say, is sheltering a brood of young, the stoat, even if it fails to catch and kill the parent bird, will probably succeed in destroying all or part of the brood. In the latter instance, mind you, I do not say that the stoat will always succeed. If it did, we should see very few partridges about the countryside. The partridge is a wonderful mother, and if she cannot lead away attacking vermin by flopping along the ground in the pretence of being wounded, she will launch a vicious attack on it, with much screaming and flapping of wings.

Nevertheless, where stoats and rats are allowed to work

the hedgerows and grassy banks where game-birds nest, many clutches of eggs will be destroyed, while it is probable that several old birds at least will be seized and killed on the nest. Therefore, it becomes perfectly clear that if good nesting-sites in the form of hedges and banks are kept clear of vermin, the birds have a far better chance of bringing off their broods, and every brood is a prospective covey. Nor are stoats and rats the only vermin that work the hedgerows and damage game prospects. The hedgehog is an inveterate egg thief as I have already shown, while the weasel, especially when she has a litter of young for which to cater, is not to be encouraged.

Before the herbage begins to grow, care should be taken to see that all rats are driven from their burrows. This may be done by ferreting, trapping and, where it is safe, poisoning. Most satisfactory of all is, perhaps, a gassing machine, manufactured for this purpose. In spring, however, there will be nothing like the number of rats in the open fields that there are when the corn is ripening and for some weeks after harvest. Rats follow the corn crops, and, when these are stored in barns, or built into stacks, the rats leave their burrows and those of rabbits, which they frequently occupy in hedges and banks, and take to the barns and stacks. All the same, there will ever be a small number of rats working the hedgerows, and for that reason traps should always be in action at strategical points on the shoot.

The most deadly, and incidentally the most simple form of trap, is the tunnel trap. Tunnel traps should be kept set in every hedgerow and bank that is likely to be used by vermin, particularly those which join a wood or copse. Of course, traps must be visited at least once every day, and if there are days, or even weeks, when a visit to them is impossible, they should not be left set. To leave vermin caught in traps to suffer and die is criminal wickedness, no less, so that if there is any doubt that traps will not be visited within

83

twenty-four hours of their being set, they should on no account be brought into action.

The tunnel trap is, as its name implies, a form of tunnel through which ground vermin is encouraged to run, but which conceals a steel trap. The tunnel itself may be made of boards, or built up with bricks, or pieces of natural wood. It should be approximately 18 in. in length, 6 in. wide and 5 in. high. If made of boards or bricks, earth and bits of stick should be heaped over it, to camouflage it so that it tones in with the hedge, bank or herbage where it is set. Some people prefer to leave a nitch in the centre of one side so that the jaws and pan of a trap may be inserted half-way along it, with the spring passing through the nitch and re-maining buried outside. I much prefer, however, to leave the tunnel undisturbed, setting the trap at one end and at a slight angle. The trap should be firmly pegged down, or wired to the hedge. The " shape " of the trap is then dug out of the ground, so that both jaws and spring are sunk a little lower than the surface. In covering the spring with earth, always make sure that the soil is pressed down firmly round it. Over the jaws and pan fine earth may be sprinkled with a sieve, or lightly " flicked " over with a twig. No small stone or piece of stick must be allowed on this end of the trap, or, when it springs, this may catch in the corner of the jaws, holding them sufficiently apart to allow vermin to escape. Or it may work itself under the pan, preventing the trap from springing easily. A few dead leaves dropped on the trap may help to camouflage it better, if the surrounding ground is so covered. Some keepers of my acquaintance leave the jaws and pan of the trap uncovered, and a certain number of vermin are caught in this way. But it is obviously better to cover the trap lightly and to camouflage it. A wary stoat, or old-stager rat might well shy at naked steel, while planting a foot on a covered trap before it realised its danger.

For the sake of causing as little suffering as possible, traps

84

with 4 in. jaws should be used for vermin catching. Smaller traps will close on the leg of the victim and certainly hold it, unless it wrenches or gnaws off the limb, but the larger jaws take the victim across the body and cause instantaneous death. Traps for vermin must be set " tittle," *i.e.* lightly, so that they spring immediately a light body passes over the pan. When young rabbits are plentiful, a number will get caught in tunnel traps, so that during the spring and summer months traps should be visited twice a day, when this is possible. No bait is required for the tunnel trap, but when, say, a stoat is caught, the body should be rubbed over the trap and the surrounding tunnel, as the scent is likely to attract others, particularly those of the other sex.

It is not uncommon to find a number of vermin proudly displayed near a tunnel trap, these being suspended from a neighbouring bush. In this way your prowess as a catcher of vermin is shown, but the display also gives away the location of the trap, with the result that interfering passers-by may steal the trap or mischievously spring it. Therefore, it is wiser to bury the vermin caught or take it away elsewhere.

Other excellent places to set tunnel traps are beside the banks of springs, between the roots of trees showing above ground and against the upturned roots of fallen trees. Stoats dearly love to play round such spots, and being thirsty little animals will often follow the bank of a stream, for here, too, they will find other creatures attracted by water. Also, by following the bank, they come eventually to a bridge, or a fallen bough, or tree by which they can cross. In time of snow it is possible to see to what great extent this practice is followed. If a plank crosses the water, a tunnel trap set under one end of it on the bank will surely take its toll, and one successful trap I worked was set among the ivy of a tree fallen across a brook. In this case, the trap was tied to a branch by a length of string that allowed the trap and its victim to fall into the brook, where death came quickly to it.

The second type of trap most used on the game preserves is known as the baited trap. But here let me issue a warning. Highly scented bait may attract dogs, which fact may lead to complications. By law, no baited trap may be set so close to a roadway, or right-of-way that it can attract a dog.

Baited traps are set against hedgerows in which partridge are nesting, beside rides in covert, or at the foot of trees. Leading from the foot of the tree, or the background of hedge or bush a " run-in " or open passage-way is formed of twigs about 6 in. high, stuck into the ground on both sides of a " shape " scratched in the ground to hold a trap. The twigs should tone in with their surroundings. At the back of the " run-in " the bait is placed, this being a tiny dead rabbit with its stomach opened out, or the paunch of a fully grown rabbit. In hot weather it is wise to change the bait daily, or the flies or maggots on it may attract birds. If, however, the bait is kept fresh, only undesirable vermin will be caught, both furred and feathered. A variety of bait may be addled eggs, or, when the weather is cold, flesh may be allowed to rot, when Prickles, the hedgehog, will be attracted. The trap set in the " run-in " must be buried, as it is in the case of the tunnel trap, the pan being lightly covered with a sprinkling of grass, or whatever material most suits the natural surroundings. If grass is used, this must be frequently changed, as it dries and becomes discoloured, or the suspicion of vermin will be roused. The point of the spring of the trap should be under the bait, so that the jaws and pan are two or three inches away from the lure and set lightly askew. Thus, any vermin directing itself towards the bait will place a foot on the pan and cause the trap to spring.

By the introduction comparatively recently of a Bill, the setting of steel traps above ground for the purpose of taking ground game was prohibited, but the setting of baited traps for vermin is not affected by this law, otherwise those who trap vermin on the game preserves and those who set traps for rats on the farm would be at a loss how to proceed in many cases and vermin would benefit accordingly.

In passing, I would make it clear that the once popular pole trap has long been made illegal, and rightly so. This consisted of a circular steel trap set on top of a pole in the ride of a wood, along a hillside, on the highest post of a fence, or even on an artificial cairn of stones. Hawks are attracted by such " roosts " and there is no doubt that of all hawk traps this was the most deadly. Unfortunately, however, it took a terrible toll of owls, particularly of the useful barn-owl and for this reason alone few regretted its passing.

Hawks may be trapped to their kills, or in special cage-traps in which a decoy is placed. They may even be caught in a trap baited with a piece of red flannel resembling flesh, or to a decoy in a wire cage with traps set round it. So complicated has the law become, however, that deals with traps and live birds in cages, that one feels that the gun is best recommended as a means of killing those hawks, the presence of which is detrimental to game. Jays, magpies, crows and rooks can be trapped to a bait of egg or flesh. Egg traps may be procured which spring as the egg is lifted from the pan of the trap.

Rabbit trapping can hardly be termed sport, but the sportsman has sometimes to " descend " to it, in order to assist in destroying rabbits damaging farm crops. I feel, therefore, that an outline of the process will not be out of place. Briefly, then, I will explain how it is done. While a professional trapper may " work " several dozen traps, the sportsman will probably be content to use only a few and to clear one burrow at a time. Let us take a burrow with twenty holes. For this perhaps, a dozen traps may suffice. Traps are set in twelve of the most-used holes, the others being firmly blocked in, so that the inmates of the burrows cannot scratch their way out, being compelled to use only the holes trapped. A " shape " is now formed as far down

87

the entrance to the hole as it is feasible to make it, allowing for the closing of the jaws of the trap. As with other forms of trapping, the jaws and pan of the trap are lightly covered with soil and earth is pressed down firmly round and over the spring. A peg is hammered into the ground, through the ring in the end of the chain, before the trap is set and that is about all there is to it. The burrow, of course, is kept trapped until cleared of rabbits.

Next morning early, a visit must be paid to the traps and the rabbits, which will be found to have drawn the traps as far down the holes as possible, taken therefrom and killed. To retrieve a rabbit from the hole down which it has pulled the trap, the hand should be inserted and the rabbit clasped firmly round the back behind the hind-legs. This saves any pain which might be inflicted by attempting to draw the trap out with the rabbit behind it.

Systematic rabbit trapping helps to keep down vermin, for the professional rabbit catcher accounts for many rats, stoats and poaching cats in the course of a season, to say nothing of odd catches such as hedgehogs and little owls. The latter may often be found down rabbit burrows, where they probably feed on insects, and also upon baby rabbits in due season.

Snaring is a great art and one which must be mastered through bitter experience. It is best learned under the practical directions of a master-hand; even then, the pupil may lack that in his " make-up " which will allow him to become as proficient in the art as he would wish.

A complete snare, of course, is made up of four separate pieces. There is (*a*) the wire noose, (*b*) the short length of cord which is attached to it and the other end of which is fixed to the peg, (*c*) the peg with its sharpened end which is driven into the ground so that it is " planted " firmly enough to hold a struggling rabbit, (*d*) the tealer, which is a thin stick, about 6 in. in length, split at one end and pointed at

88

the other, its object being to hold up the snare and cock it at the correct angle.

Sometimes I am approached by an individual who produces a snare from his pocket and asks me to show him the proper size and shape to make a wire, and then questions how far off the ground it should be set, and at what angle. The fact that I fashion the wire into a small pear-shaped noose that I prefer, and explain that roughly four fingers from the ground should make the thin end of the " pear " and that the wire should be cocked at just this angle seems to satisfy him. He takes the wire, shapes the " pear " after a lot of fumbling and thinks he has " got the idea."

Now as to the proper place to set a wire. Should it be set close to the fence, or as far out in the field as possible ? Will it do to set it anywhere in a well-defined run ? The last of these questions is, perhaps, the easier to answer, but, here again, without practical experience and a good " snarer's eye," it is doubtful whether one in six snares would be placed " just so." Your experienced snarer talks about and well understands " jumps." They show him those places along a run where a hopping rabbit lands with its front feet, and if the snare is set " just so " in a " jump," is the right height from the ground and cocked at the right angle, then it will serve its purpose. A really clever snarer will find a great many of his rabbits dead, for his small wire, catching the rabbit in front of the ears, will push back the head and dislocate the neck.

As to how far out in a field or meadow you set your wires, no definite rule can be laid down in this respect. You may tell a man to set his wires from twenty-five to fifty yards out from a covert, or fence, but the fact is that every field or meadow differs and there are also other matters to bear in mind. If foxes are plentiful, for instance, you may lose a good proportion of your catch if the snares are out in a line across a track taken by foxes on their nocturnal rambles.

There is one wood especially that comes to mind. Snares set in the big meadow outside seemed to attract foxes and the rabbits caught in these could be written off as a dead loss. The only way in which one could be certain of making a catch was to set the wires in runs inside the wood. This may seem strange procedure, but it sometimes pays.

The professional snarer likes to run out his wires in lines. By doing this he saves a lot of time when going his rounds. He has only to walk in a line to catch a glimpse of each wire and see that it remains properly set and has not been knocked down, or brushed on one side. To zigzag about ground in search of wires not only takes up valuable time, but snares are all too easy to overlook. Sometimes, of course, a dead line cannot be kept, for there are spots not to be missed just out of " true," but certainly a line of snares should be as straight as possible.

The amateur snarer will take time to set up each wire, having to go down on at least one knee to do so. There are experts that never need to kneel when the ground is reasonably soft. The peg can be heeled into the ground and the tealer stuck in and the wire cocked almost in one movement. This also saves much time if you are running out a couple of hundred wires. To smooth out kinks in a used wire, hold it taut and run the tealer up and down it.

The trapping and snaring of rats round stackyards and farm buildings is a fascinating business. I need not, I think, detail the methods by which rats can be trapped, except to emphasise that traps should be concealed, either by earth or chaff and some sort of protection built round and over them so that poultry and cats do not suffer.

The snaring of rats is not quite so simple, but, once mastered, is both good fun and an efficient way of catching them as they use their well-defined runs along banks, or between, say, stacks and drinking-places in a nearby ditch. To snare rats, whether it be in the fields, or round the farm, fine wire is necessary. A running noose is formed and sufficient length of wire left to bind one end a couple of inches from the top of a supple stick (named a " bender ") of from 3½ ft. to 4 ft. in length. Into the ground, to one side of the run, a small peg is hammered which has a notch cut near the top, the notch being almost flush with the ground. A similar notch is cut near the top of the " bender " and when the " bender " is forced into the ground some way on the other side of the run and bent half hoop-shape, the two notches come together and fix lightly into each other and the noose of the wire is then set, not pear-shape as a rabbit snare, but round, and adjusted over the run. No tealer is necessary. A rat passing hurriedly along the run, with its mind on possible enemies, such as cats and owls, will slip its head through the noose, when the jerk occasioned causes the notch in the " bender " to slip from the notch in the peg, with the result that the " bender " will fly up and straighten and the rat will be suspended in mid-air.

At one time, when farmers willingly paid 2d. each for rats caught, I made a respectable sum of pocket-money as a result of shooting, trapping and snaring them. But whether rats are killed for gain or not, every one of these rodents laid low is a good turn accomplished, both to the farmer and to any one interested in game.

It might be thought that the mole is a comparatively harmless creature where game is concerned, but moles should be trapped on and in the vicinity of pheasant-rearing fields, or weasels will use their runs and pheasant chicks will be found mysteriously to disappear as they are killed in the long grass and pulled down the runs.

Nor should moles be encouraged in the vicinity of partridge nests, for this is what sometimes happens. The old partridge, sitting on her eggs, goes off the nest to feed in the early morning, when the dew is on the herbage. She returns to the nest with her plumage damp, which no doubt is an excellent thing for the eggs, which need damping. However, this damp, and the warmth of the bird's body, draws earth-worms to the ground directly beneath the eggs, and after the earth-worms comes their deadly enemy the mole.

On more than one occasion I have known burrowing moles to tunnel under the eggs, so that the latter fell through into the mole's run, there to be pushed and shoved along it by the mole in the course of its passage. It is surprising the number of eggs that a mole can push along its run, and it must be very strong and something of a juggler to perform the feat. On one occasion, having rescued a number of eggs from a mole run, I stamped this in, and after inserted something unpleasant which I knew would keep the mole away. I built up the nest (if such the scrape of a partridge can be called) and hoped that the old bird, who was sitting hard on a second and small clutch, would return to her duties. I am glad to record that she did this and that the eggs hatched, but it was no thanks to the mole that a small covey occupied that field in due course.

Publisher's Note

Some parts of this chapter on trapping and snaring refer to practices which are now illegal. However, they are of historical interest as a record of bygone methods and have therefore been retained. The detailed survey of the changes in this area since this chapter was written can be found in the editor's preface of the third edition on page xiii.

CHAPTER TEN

Ferreting

Care and Management of Ferrets—Handling and Working—When Rabbits Bolt—When Rabbits will not Bolt—Purse Netting—" Lay-ups "—Recovering Lost Ferrets—Muzzled Ferrets.

FERRETS, in their habits, are among the cleanest animals I know. Kept in dry, warm hutches, which should be frequently cleaned, they rarely foul their beds, but repair to a corner of the outer hutch to attend to their natural functions. For this reason, I favour a hutch divided into two compartments. In the smaller inside compartment a liberal amount of oat-straw or hay should be placed for a bed and, though some people seem to prefer straw litter for the outer compartment, I much prefer a covering of peat-moss or even sawdust. This soaks up any liquid and should be removed at least three times a week. A number of holes should be bored in the wooden floor (I do not hold with a wire-netting floor, which quickly gets caked up with undesirable matter), particularly in the corner of the compartment most used by the ferrets. A sprinkling of insect powder to prevent invasion of vermin is very important, especially in the sleeping compartment which should not require cleaning out nearly so often as the outside portion of the hutch. If ferrets are properly fed twice a day (*i.e.* given just as much as they can eat), they will not leave odd bits of food in their nest, to become rapidly putrid in hot weather. Scrupulous cleanliness is the keynote to successful ferret-keeping. Fed and well looked after there will be little danger of their acquiring foot-rot and other troubles which are common among ferrets kept in dirty hutches and given all too little of that consideration which is their due.

Feeding is the next most important matter in the management of ferrets, for upon this to a very great extent depends their working qualities which may mean all the difference between good or poor sport. " Feed your ferrets well and they will never lay-up " is common enough advice. Less frequently we hear " Don't give your ferrets any food before you take them out ; they'll hunt all the better." I will admit that there is a certain amount of logic in both camps of thought, but, in practice, neither piece of advice is worth following in its entirety.

The ferret is a carnivorous animal and a diet composed almost entirely of bread and milk is not only unsuitable to it, but may help to lower its stamina, a thing to be avoided in a little animal of which a great deal of tiring work is expected in due season. By all means allow bread and milk to form the main item of diet, particularly in the " close " season, but certainly ferrets should have a reasonable supply of such food as small birds, bits of rabbit, heads and necks of poultry and young rats that are free from disease. This latter point is important, as ferrets are prone to disease of the skin, and many of the rats we kill show all too clearly that they are suffering from some form of mange.

Ferrets, then, should be fed as common sense and observation dictate. A little more meat at the time of the year when they are being worked is all to the good, and, if they are provided with this for the evening meal, a light breakfast of bread and milk before taking them out is, I think, an ideal form of rationing. It should be remembered that a hungry ferret, when it kills a rabbit in the burrow, will stay with it and have a good feed while its owner waits, impatient and perhaps half-frozen, for it to put in an appearance, or finds himself digging when he would rather be using the gun. On the other hand, an over-fed ferret will tend to become lazy and will quickly tire—perhaps just at a time when rabbits are plentiful and are bolting well.

There is no doubt that the ferret is much misunderstood, both as regards feeding and handling. Consequently, it has gained a reputation for " snappiness " it does not deserve. Ferrets, from the time when they make their first appearance to feed in the outer compartment of the hutch, should be handled as much as possible. It is a sorry sight to watch a man go to his ferret hutches to collect the empty tins, doing so by a series of quick snatches which show that he does not trust his own ferrets. A pleasant and enlightening sight is to watch an owner fearlessly open the door of the hutch and gently take out the tin, what time the inmates scramble about his hands. By constant and fearless handling, ferrets become as tame—indeed a good deal tamer—than domestic cats and kittens. They learn to know and to love the hand that feeds them and will come straight to it from the mouth of the burrow instead of lingering or " drawing back " as do those which have been roughly or foolishly handled. Ferrets can be both affectionate and intelligent, and those that have been carefully looked after, well handled and show an appreciation of such treatment by doing good work for their owners, cannot be too highly valued. It is too easy to have a day's sport spoiled through using ferrets that kill often, lay-up for long periods, tire easily and are difficult to pick up at the mouth of the hole.

Whether white ferrets or polecat ferrets are the better workers is a matter of opinion, and also a matter of individual ferrets. There are good and bad workers of both kinds. I think the average polecat ferret retains a slightly more wild nature than the white ; the few polecat ferrets that I have lost for days became markedly more wild than white ones that have escaped. Polecats also seem to hunt with more natural vigour and often show more ferocity towards their prey. In short, it has always seemed to me that the true polecat ferret retains more of the instincts of its wild ancestors than does the white. I have owned many small polecat ferrets that were ideal ratters, but for rabbiting I have a marked preference for the white ferret, and it has the decided advantage that it is more easily seen in thick cover.

Most young sportsmen who keep ferrets are keen to breed from their best workers. This is not a difficult matter, but there are one or two points that should be made clear. The period of gestation of the ferret is about six weeks. When in season, the bitch should be placed with the dog, which is kept in a separate hutch, on two occasions, on two consecutive days. I err, perhaps, in referring to the male and female ferret as dog and bitch, when the proper terms are hob and jill, but the fact is that the latter terms, though strictly correct, are far less used than the popular dog and bitch—which appellations apply also to the stoat.

The young ferrets born in May and averaging six to ten in a litter, are blind for the first six weeks of their lives, but even before their eyes are fully open they will make regular appearance in the outer hutch, to feed with their mother. No disturbance to the breeding compartment of the hutch should be made for five or six weeks after the young are born ; otherwise it will be found that mother ferret has a nasty habit of devouring her young. It is, I know, a great temptation to open the door of the inner compartment when the old ferret is feeding in the outer, just to have a peep at the nestlings, and, if possible, gain some idea of their number. A kindly ferret may not eat her young but the risk taken to satisfy the curiosity is a big one and certainly not worth while. At ten weeks old, the young can be weaned, when, for a time, they should be fed three or four times a day. Weaklings should be killed, or kept in isolation hutches, for they may start an epidemic of distemper, a complaint that all too

Loading up

Young shots observing safety principles

often makes inroads among the litters. Warmth and cleanliness of the hutches must never be neglected, and the young ferrets may now be allowed to crawl over the hand that feeds them, being picked up and gently handled, so that in future they will not regard the advancing human form, or the outstretched hand as something to be feared.

The paraphernalia for an ordinary " small " day's ferreting is simple. Three ferrets are sufficient, though in anticipation of a serious " lay-up " it is perhaps as well to take four if one is going far from home. One of these, the strong dog ferret, trained to wear a collar to which is attached a lengthy cord or line, should be carried in a separate box or bag.

The object of the " liner," or cord-ferret is to discover the whereabouts of any loose ferret which happens to have made a kill, or is scratching at the rump of an obstinate rabbit that has hunched itself up in a dead-end and refuses to turn and bolt. The " liner " being bigger and stronger than the loose ferret, which is usually a bitch, generally manages to make a kill, or, if the loose ferret has already killed, will stay with her and feed. A light pull on the line will give the dog the impression that he is being dragged from his food, and, feeling that such treatment is hardly playing the game, he will seize the victim and hold on for grim death. If the rabbit is fairly close, and the hole is a comparatively straight one, it is sometimes possible by gentle and judicious pulling to bring both ferret and rabbit to the surface. More often, however, the kill is far down a twisting hole and it is then that digging operations must commence. For these a graft or spade is necessary, and some ferreters carry a thin iron rod which can be used as a probe in order to discover the direction which the hole takes.

It is a moot point whether one carries the ferrets in boxes or sacks, but whichever are used they should contain a handful or two of straw or hay, to keep the ferrets warm and dry. Strong canvas bags may be obtained, with ventilation holes round the neck and a cord for tying attached. If an ordinary sack is used, it must be neither too thin nor too thick. If it is thin, the ferrets will probably bite a hole in it and escape ; if too thick, they may suffer from lack of reasonable ventilation. A piece of string should be threaded through and tied below the mouth of the sack, for often one is in a hurry to put in or take out a ferret, and then to have to search for a dropped bit of loose string can be very irritating.

A box containing ferrets not in use should never be placed too near to the burrow, for ferrets anxious to be out, and scratching against the sides or lid make a noise that may easily be the means of scaring a listening rabbit about to bolt.

Apart from the ferrets and the graft, a shoulder bag is required in which to carry the purse nets, the collar and line for the cord-ferret and any small accessories, such as a little bottle of milk for the ferrets or even a mid-day snack for the sportsmen. Equipped thus, with the addition of gun and cartridge bag, the expedition is ready to set out, and let us hope that there is good sport in the offing.

It is a popular belief that rabbits bolt best on a cold, crisp morning when there is a bone in the ground. To a certain extent this is true, although I have had many first-rate days when weather conditions were just the reverse. I think, myself, that the worst ferreting days are those when heavy rain has fallen and the trees and bushes are dripping wet and a cold wind soughs across the burrows.

Calm frosty mornings are certainly the most attractive for ferreting, but they also have their handicaps—handicaps that may be overcome by those who learn from experience the ways of rabbits and rabbit architecture.

I do not think it is necessary for me to stress the fact that one should where possible, stand downwind to the burrow in which ferrets have been entered. The scent of ferret along the corridors of the burrow will throw rabbits into a panic and instinctively they come to the surface with the object of making good their escape. But rabbits, despite their fear and natural nervousness, are by no means fools. A protective instinct goes far to guide them when they are not too hard pushed. I think anyone who has done much ferreting will agree with me that rabbits are capable of quite a lot of cool reasoning. Unless a ferret is close on their heels, I doubt whether many rabbits bolt from their burrows without first stopping just down the mouth of a hole, or even just outside it, to listen and " smell the air." I have seen scores of rabbits intending to make a bolt for it, first stop at the mouth of the hole, listen intently, noses working hard ; they are taxed with the problem of discovering how close is the dreaded ferret, but also if the coast outside is clear. Thus, if the sportsman is standing downwind, the nose of the rabbit is incapable of scenting him and if he stands rigid and absolutely motionless, neither the ears nor the eyes of the rabbit will discern him. Imagining itself to be in a position to make a clean getaway, and probably thanking its lucky stars for this opportunity of escape, the hunted rabbit will now dash off across the open to another burrow of its knowing, or slip cunningly along one of its well-worn runs in the undergrowth, when a cleverly directed charge of shot may hit it in the head and send it somersaulting to lie, one more rabbit for the bag, among a scurry of fallen leaves.

When a bone is in the ground, and the spade rings as it comes into contact with the iron-hard earth, when the frost still sparkles in the weak winter sunlight, then, though we are told rabbits should bolt well, we sometimes find that the reverse is the case, and we wonder why. Often, it is our own faults. We forget that sound carries and is magnified several-fold under the circumstances. Rabbits resting in their burrows after a night of feeding hear approaching footfalls, hear the low murmur of voices, perhaps even scent the aroma of tobacco as a gentle draught creeping down the burrows carries the tell-tale warning. It may be argued that horses and cattle walking about in the meadow above may equally scare the rabbits, or, if such is not the case, then that the tramp of human feet could not be distinguished from that of farm animals. However, I do not propose to discourse further on this rather involved question, but I do know, from long experience, that on quiet days, when the ground is hard, the greatest care should be taken not to walk over the burrows, to whisper as little as possible and, when entering the ferrets, to do so quickly and quietly. When purse nets are to be set over the holes, this warning is doubly necessary, for creeping from hole to hole, kneeling and rising from the ground, removing growth from about the holes and getting the peg of the net home, all tend towards issuing a warning to sharp ears below ground.

At all times ferreting should be carried out with the minimum of noise and disturbance, and once the ferrets are entered, those with guns, or those waiting to pounce on rabbits bolting into nets, should keep as still and silent as possible. Many a hard hour's digging has been due to some tiny movement, perhaps the slight raising of the gun barrels, just as a rabbit has looked out from a hole. That quick eye has immediately registered danger unknown, and in a flash the rabbit has doubled back in fear into the hole, only to be caught by a ferret that proceeds to make the best of its opportunities and probably eats its fill and then settles down for a sleep beside its victim.

For the ferreting of rabbits in thick cover, where, of necessity, the sportsman must stand near the holes and kill his rabbits at short ranges, the little ·410 is the most useful weapon. It does not " smash " the rabbits as must a gun of larger bore, shooting a heavier charge of shot. One cannot see far ahead among beds of nettles, for instance, and here the smaller bore is definitely more satisfactory than the usual 12-bore. No. 6 shot is my ideal for this kind of close shooting although I do not condemn the use of No. 7 shot if one can be certain that few rabbits will be shot beyond, say, twenty yards.

There are times when it seems almost necessary and quite safe to shoot rabbits on the burrow itself, but the general rule should be to let them get away. I have seen more than one ferret, coming suddenly out of a hole, meet part of a charge of shot meant for a rabbit and so become entitled to mention with the day's bag ! A rabbit away from the burrow may unfortunately be wounded, and a second barrel can then finish its career, or a dog be sent in to catch it. If, however, it was hit while on the burrow, it is ten to one that it will escape down one of the holes, to fall an easy victim to a ferret, and so cause a lay-up.

When a single gun is ferreting, it is sometimes wise to place a net or two over bolt-holes on the far side of the hedge. One cannot be on both sides of a fence at the same time, but it may be only the work of a minute to slip through a gap in the hedge and despatch a rabbit struggling in a net.

And take warning from a very old story. There were once two men who went ferreting on a bitter cold day. After twenty minutes of standing with frozen feet and numbed fingers on their respective sides of a thick hedge, they decided that the ferret had killed and that the line-ferret ought to be introduced. Accordingly, the man who had the ferret boxes on his side, walked over to fetch the " liner." After several minutes of struggling to fix the collar with fingers that seemed twice their normal size, he approached the burrow and called to his friend, " Which hole did you put the loose ferret in ? " " Who, me ? " came the reply, " I didn't put in any ferret ; I thought you had done so." Of course, the ferret was found snugly sleeping in its box.

Purse netting is an art in itself, but one that it is not difficult to master, if you remember the rules of silence and stealth. True, it is unavoidable sometimes to crack twigs and make a certain amount of disturbance when kneeling on ground that is covered with dried sticks, or when clearing a hole of growth so that the net can be properly set. The tiniest bit of twig caught in the meshes of a net will cause valuable time to be lost while it is being disentangled. Consequently, clear the ground round the hole of bits and pieces likely to interfere with the net, and see that the peg is firmly pushed into the ground and the string tied to some sound hold such as a strong root, or a stump. Press the edges of the net into the earth with a thumb, so that a slight hold is given to them as the rabbit dashes into the purse, and mind that no gaps are left between the net and the sides of the hole. Bolt holes, or " pop-holes " as they are sometimes called, need special care. Having no scratched-out earth to mark them, they are often overlooked, and sometimes a merry little breeze has covered them with dead leaves. These the rabbits use most when leaving their burrows, particularly in an emergency.

Properly fed ferrets seldom lay-up for long. They may kill, but they quickly leave the dead rabbit and, with the natural instinct of hunters, set off in pursuit of others. However, really good ferrets of this kind are by no means common, and lay-ups from time to time are inevitable.

When it has been decided that it is time to enter the line-ferret, first of all try it down the hole where the loose ferret was released ; unless, of course, you can, after putting an ear to several holes, hear the ferret scratching at a rabbit, or the rabbit squealing. In that case, enter the " liner " at the nearest hole to the sound. A knot tied in the line a foot from the collar, and two more knots tied at intervals of two feet up the cord, will be of great assistance as digging continues, for then on finding these knots one can tell exactly how far off the seat of the trouble lies.

With the " liner " entered, try and " feel " or sense the

direction it is taking and how far in it goes. Once it has reached the dead or " tucked up " rabbit and the loose ferret, allow it to get a firm grip on its victim, and then with the aid of a pliable stick, or a bramble, attempt to learn the course the line has taken and break into the hole as far away as possible from that down which the " liner " has gone. This may save a lot of unnecessary digging. If, as is frequently the case, however, the line twists and turns among a labyrinth of corridors, it may be necessary to follow it by digging out the hole foot by foot along which it runs. Experience soon teaches you the best and quickest way to come on to the trouble and recover your ferrets.

There are times when the " liner," for some strange reason, fails absolutely to discover the kill. Or perhaps he is tired, bored, or over-fed and prefers his box to working. There is not much to be done then, except to take a stick and rattle down various holes, and bang on the surface with the flat of the spade in the hope that the erring ferret's interest will be attracted. If there is a rabbit or two handy, these can be opened and paunched and pegged down near holes upwind of the burrow. A paunch may be placed at the entrance to one, and the " fumes " from it fanned down the hole with the aid of a hat. In the days of black powder, it used to be a dodge to extract the shots from a cartridge and fire down the hole, but I never found this answered well in any but small burrows. There are fuses that can be bought and set alight in burrows, that are supposed to bolt rabbits or ferrets. I have not tried these myself, but friends who have done so do not speak too highly of their effect.

If one does much ferreting it is useful to have some form of box-trap or wire-cage that can be left on the burrow when a ferret has not shown up before dark. In this case all holes should be blocked up, save the one at which the trap is set. Personally, I either block in all holes and return next morning at daybreak, or, sometimes, I leave one hole open and place the ferret sack with straw in it at the mouth, the latter kept open with a stick. It is rarely that ferrets are lost for long, for, if they scratch their way out of a burrow that has been blocked up, they will soon be seen by some farm-hand, or passer-by, and their whereabouts reported. Some ferrets get wild very quickly; others remain comparatively tame after a week of freedom, but it is always advisable to handle such animals with care, and to remove all ticks from them before returning them to their hutch.

When digging for a ferret, particularly in sandy or light soil, great care should be taken not to wound it with the spade, or block it in with a fall of earth. This sometimes happens, and then one is fortunate ever to see the ferret again. Likewise, a ferret sometimes gets blocked up in a dead-end by rabbits that it has killed and over which it has crawled to reach the farthest. Sometimes it can eat, or scratch its way out of the difficulty, but not always.

Single holes, or dead-end holes of burrows occasionally offer rich rewards after the efforts of digging. I remember a few seasons ago trying out a single hole with a line ferret. This hole was found to be seven yards in length, but ran downwards through stiff clay at a sharp angle. It also ran under the roots of an ash tree. It took nearly an hour of hard digging before I came on the welcome sight of the ferret's tail. Slipping my hand along its back, I placed my thumb on the top of its head and my first finger under its lower jaw and pressed gently—the best and surest way to force a ferret to let go its hold. In that dead-end were no less than nine rabbits and, though a good deal of heavy digging was still necessary, the work seemed lighter and lighter as each rabbit was brought to the surface and quickly despatched. Never leave a dead-end until you can feel with your hand that it is empty, or the " liner " tells you that there are no more rabbits in it. Also, when you are pulling rabbits out of such a place, keep one foot over the hole while you are despatching a rabbit, or others may bolt and make you feel that you would like to kick yourself none too gently.

There are those who believe in muzzling ferrets, either with string or with metal muzzles that may be bought for the purpose. It is true that ferrets can be trained to work well with muzzles and there is no chance of a lay-up. But do they work so well and so keenly as ferrets that are free to catch and kill? I am certain they do not. Moreover, they must leave many rabbits in dead-ends that the feel of their teeth might have moved, but which remain obstinate before their attacker's claws. There is another point. A ferret may come face to face with other things than rabbits and, though a fox, an otter, a poaching cat and even a stoat will probably bolt without showing fight, an old buck rat, or even a doe with young will not hesitate to face a ferret and inflict serious injuries upon it—injuries that are often poisonous and prove fatal.

It would not be a difficult task to write a whole book on ferrets and ferreting, for he who has spent a great deal of time at the game has many stories to relate and many dodges to unfold. I imagine, however, that in this chapter I have covered the subject sufficiently to show those who are new to the sport how to go about it and have laid enough emphasis upon those rules of stealth and silence, the neglect of which can only lead to countless disappointing outings.

CHAPTER ELEVEN

Pigeon Shooting—I

The Pigeon in Sport—Recognising the Species—Food and Characteristics—The Effects of Migration on Sport —Pigeon Craft—Hides and How to Build Them.

THERE can be few more fascinating forms of sport with the gun than that which develops round pigeon shooting. To be able to kill good bags of pigeon under the very great variety of circumstances which present themselves through the seasons, not only calls for more than ordinary skill and practice, but these must be combined with a profound knowledge of the ways and feeding habits of the birds and the best methods to adopt as opportunity occurs. Pigeon, where much shot at, rapidly become wary and if their eyesight is not quite so quick as that of crows, rooks and hawks, it should never be underrated. The sudden showing of a face, the jerking up of the gun, the glint of sunlight on gun-barrels, in fact any movement or unusual sight that is liable to attract sharp eyes, is all sufficient to set birds hitherto flying on a straight line, swerving and dodging to the consternation of the shooter and to the detriment of his shooting.

From October to January, our resident stock of pigeon is greatly augmented by the arrival of migratory birds. Vast flocks visit us from across the North Sea, remaining here until the end of February, when the return migration is undertaken. These " foreign " pigeon are rather smaller and darker than those hatched over here, but are otherwise difficult to identify from the wood-pigeon, or ring-dove to give it its proper name, that has been bred and remains in the British Isles. The ring-dove, the largest of our pigeon, can, apart from its size, be easily identified by the white patch on its neck and the white bars on the outstretched wings. Far more common than other species, it can truly be described as a serious pest to farmers, most of whom are only too glad to give permission to bona fide pigeon shooters to kill the birds that are damaging their crops. In the event of the game shooting being let, permission should also be sought from the shooting tenant or his keeper, who, if he feels that the applicant will confine himself to certain specified spots and will take care not to disturb the game, is often ready not only to grant him his wish, but may tell him where the pigeon are feeding, their lines of flight, or the best stands to take up as the birds fly in to roost in the evening.

The second most common pigeon is the stock-dove, a smaller bird altogether than the ring-dove and one which seems to have quicker eyesight than the latter and is certainly wilder and more active on wing when danger presents itself. To my mind, this bird is even more attractive, from a sporting point of view, than the " woodie," for, apart from the fact that it may be said to be comparatively scarce when compared with the vast hordes of resident and migratory ring-doves, it is more restless when feeding in flocks, more wary and its manner of flight when disturbed is such that it will tax even the best of shots.

I have enjoyed much sport when these birds are nesting in pollard willows, by walking quietly up to the trees and then shooting them as they come darting out. It is, however, a matter for contention whether this bird should be shot when nesting. It does not do nearly so much harm to agriculture as does the wood-pigeon, and therefore, for humane reasons, it might be thought justifiable to allow it a close time in which to breed. On the same grounds, some people defend the wood-pigeon, but those opposed to giving this pest any respite, ask if the rat, which also has its feelings, should not be protected when breeding in case young are allowed to starve in the nest. Since rats breed all the year round, it is obvious that we cannot afford to consider them from a " humane " point of view, but wood-pigeon, although they nest freely in spring and summer, are also found breeding in autumn and even occasional winter nests are discovered, so that here we have another agricultural pest round which the " humane " question revolves. With other sportsmen, I have given this question a great deal of consideration, and have arrived at the following views. We cannot, in the interests of our national food supplies, afford to protect the rat, and my personal view is that the same rule must apply to the wood-pigeon. The stock-dove, on the other hand, although it consumes a certain amount of corn and green stuff, is also a great eater of weeds and weed-seed and, since it is neither so numerous nor so prolific as its larger cousin, I would grant it a reprieve during a reasonable breeding period. However, since it must always be the golden rule of sportsmen to cause as little suffering as possible, we should try to kill the wood-pigeon, when shot during the nesting season, either when the female is laying, or sitting on eggs. If she is shot when young are in the nest, every endeavour should be made to destroy those young, either by poking them from their platform of twigs with a stick (not with the gun-barrels, as I have so often seen it accomplished !) or by firing a charge of shot into the nest.

I do not think these points have been raised before in any book dealing with sport, but they are important and will help us to uphold a sound principle.

Since the rock-dove is of similar size and appearance to the stock-dove, except that it has a white rump and clearly marked black bars on its wings, whereas the rump of the stock-dove is grey and the wing-bars are incomplete, it is not surprising that the average countryman refers to stock-doves

as " little blue rocks." In fact, the rock-dove seldom leaves
the coast-line, except to feed in adjoining fields, and here its
main food consists of weeds and weed-seed and accordingly
it may be said to do more good than harm to farm lands.
From this bird is descended our domestic breeds of pigeon
and it will freely resort and feed with them in proximity to
its natural haunts. It is said of the rock-pigeon that it is the
most sporting of them all and certainly as it arrows along the
cliff-face, or darts from holes in the cliffs, it offers a target
that even the best shots cannot despise. On the cliffs at
Flamborough Head, for instance, friends of mine enjoy the
thrill of hiding in " butts " set below the edge of the precipitous cliffs and from such vantage points shoot the pigeon
as they swerve and dive about the cliff-face, having been put
on wing by men with a good knowledge of dangerous places.
Perhaps the acme of difficult shooting is that enjoyed from a
boat on a choppy sea, when rock-doves dart from the holes
in the cliffs or rush in small flocks from the caves. Then, to
kill your birds with any consistency all too often remains a
happy dream, though the sport offered is such that one would
like to return to it again and again.

Apart from the three species of pigeon I have mentioned,
a paragraph or two must be written concerning one of our
latest migrants of spring—the turtle-dove. Of this bird,
my friend Mr. Max Baker, author of *Sport with Wood-pigeons*,
has written : " The turtle dove of proverbial innocence is
one of the greatest frauds in the realm of Nature. Not only
is it a greedy thief of corn but, like the rook, it lands to feed
on the shocks instead of availing itself of the plentiful supplies
strewn on the ground. One hundred grains is a normal
crop-load. Two meals a day for an average of twenty-five
doves frequenting a ten-acre field of oats is a costly entertain-
ment, to say the least. Where the dove escapes censure is
that it departs early in the autumn to the scorched plains of
the East—in a word, it does not destroy winter forage

crops. Its soothing note is perhaps more expressive of rural peacefulness than any other sound that reaches the ear."

Now there are many sportsmen who would never raise their guns to a turtle-dove, but, with Mr. Max Baker, who has been courageous enough to " show up " this dove in a new light, I am convinced that the reason arises almost entirely from pure sentiment. The dove is the emblem of peace ; the gentle crooning note of the turtle dove issuing from the shady trees of summer echoes in the songs of poets and the naturalist-sense of the sportsman is responsive. The turtle-dove, however, arrives in this country towards the end of April in large numbers, and I have seen big flocks of these birds feeding on valuable corn, day after day.

I have waited in the flight-line between two favoured feeding-grounds and have enjoyed first-rate sport as little lots of the birds periodically flew from one field to the other. Their rapid, arrowing flight comes to a sudden end as a shot is fired, and then to get a bird, with the second barrel, that is giving a display of aerobatics which would shame a frightened snipe, takes real skill. It is in late afternoon, at about the time when most of the corn has been carted, that these birds seem to flight regularly over a period that may last for half an hour. I have watched a boy empty a box of twenty-five cartridges within less than an hour and I have prided myself that, under my supervision, he has obtained some excellent shooting practice, for on-coming or crossing shots are not too difficult with the first barrel, and, whether rightly or wrongly, I have not allowed him to use a second barrel (which I certainly consider would cause him to shoot wildly) until he has become cool in his shooting and somewhat proficient in his performance. I may stand condemned in the eyes of older sportsmen, and naturalists pure and simple, for thus deliberately placing the turtle-dove in the category of sporting birds, but I do so only after a wide study of their habits and a cool survey of the general situation. I will add that this bird is an asset to any dining-room table.

Having outlined the different species of pigeon to be met with in the British Isles, I will return to the ring-dove and make it the pattern for the subject matter of this chapter. I have so far purposely omitted mention in any detail of its food, although it may at first be thought by young sportsmen that this can have little bearing on the subject of pigeon shooting. Actually, however, study of the bird's food at different seasons very intimately concerns the would-be successful pigeon shooter.

Long before the arrival of the pigeon legions from across the North Sea, our home-bred birds are raiding farm crops. In late summer, for instance, the bean and pea field will attract the flocks from afar. Pigeon are particularly fond of beans and peas and quantities of spilled beans and peas will be left in the field as an attractive source of food supply, until such time when the ploughs get to work and bury what are left. At this period, too, if rough winds and heavy rains have damaged the standing crops, leaving them what is known as " laid " (*i.e.* areas flattened to the ground) rooks and pigeon will descend on such damage and play havoc with the ripening ears. Newly planted kale and cabbage are also attacked and their tops eaten. At harvest time, when the corn is cut and the sheaves stand shocked, pigeon will arrive first thing in the morning and again during the latter part of the afternoon to settle on and about the sheaves, filling their crops almost to bursting point on the ripe grain. With the harvest carted, the open stubble fields are searched for the grain that has been left behind, for certain weeds and for the leaves of young clover.

By late October, smaller flocks have joined up and big droves of pigeon migrate to where a harvest of acorns, beech-mast and sweet-chestnuts litter the ground, and it is now that one begins to notice a great increase of birds, for the advance-guard of " foreign " pigeon arrive on these shores, hungry after their long flight and possible privation suffered as winter has descended on their breeding-grounds in northern Europe and Asia and food supplies become precarious. As only comparatively few " foreigners " arrive at the end of October, the bigger flocks augmenting them in November and December, most of the acorns and beech-mast have been cleared up when the invasion occurs. Also, hard weather has now probably set in and so the winter population of pigeon are forced to descend on the valuable green crops of farmer and market gardener and only those who have seen fields completely stripped by these pests can realise the immense amount of damage done annually by the British wood-pigeon and its relations from overseas. Turnip-tops, clover and " green-stuff " form the winter standby of the pigeon armies, and though such a varied diet as haws, holly and ivy berries, the seeds of charlock, tares, vetches, speedwell and bird's-eye and even small snails collected in the water-meadows are also eaten in large quantities, there is no doubt that the good done by the ring-dove is far outweighed by the damage that accrues to important agricultural crops.

Now, the importance of making a study of the food of the pigeon and of deciding that which is most likely to be popular at the moment, lies in the fact that the sportsman need not waste time sitting in a ditch or in a hide waiting for pigeon at a spot to which they are not likely to come. Yesterday, there was a big flock feeding on this pea field, but since they had been feeding here for many days, there is not likely to be many peas left, while judging by the direction taken of birds seen in flight, they are probably interesting themselves in that bit of laid corn over the brow of the hill. Then, one day, somebody remarks that all the pigeon seem to have disappeared and the usual surprise is shown. At the same time, someone else is ordering cartridges in his nearby town, for the pigeon flocks have arrived in the beech woods of his area and good sport will be obtained until the last of the beech-mast has disappeared.

A comprehensive study of " pigeon seasons " and of local crops, not only saves waste of time in attempting to locate where pigeon are feeding, but their next feeding-ground may often be anticipated and the sportsman can then forestall the flocks by preparing hides in readiness for sport he hopes to enjoy.

In the next chapter, I have gone fairly fully into the art of building hides, in the harvest field, in the flight-line of pigeon, where decoys are set out and on the various other occasions when some form of artificial concealment is necessary. The general rule in building hides, be they for wildfowl, pigeon, vermin, or merely for reasons of observation, should be to make the material used tone in with the surroundings. For instance, a hide constructed of withered boughs and rushes (or boughs and rushes that will quickly wither) must show up to the sharp eyes of birds if it is built against a background of fresh green herbage. Wary birds will notice it and pass wide of it, and this is especially the case where the birds in question know the surrounding countryside and are not passing migrants. And, if they have been shot at from such a hide, they will not only tend to pass wide of it, but will avoid it like the plague, for it has, in their minds, the double danger of something that looks artificial and is also something which they recall instinctively as a menace to their safety. Even in the harvest field, where hides are built of the sheaves themselves, pigeon are often wary of a spot from which much shooting has occurred, and, since, at that time, there are large areas of shocked corn, they are not foolish enough to risk danger unnecessarily.

As opposed to this, in hard, severe weather, when snow covers the ground, or frost has deprived them of all food save berries and greens, I have erected a hide of hurdles and sacking bang in the centre of a patch of turnip-tops, and pigeon have arrived within shot at odd intervals throughout the day.

It is then, however, a state of semi-starvation that undermines their natural caution and such a hide, erected on the day of shooting, would prove of little value under normal conditions. It is also true that a hide of this kind may, for a time, be satisfactory if it has been erected for a week or two before a shot is fired from it. Pigeon have gradually become used to it, and since they have had no reason to suspect danger, they may feed within range of it. But once a few shots are fired from it, they quickly realise that it is a " landmark " to be avoided, and will in future feed well out of range, or avoid that patch of turnips altogether.

The art of hide-building, then, is to study the art of natural camouflage ; to renew material that has died or faded, so that it tones in with the background. This goes for every kind of hide, and, though a certain number of birds may be shot from one that is not all it should be, it should be re-membered that many more birds would probably offer sport if trouble was taken to study the foregoing points.

The shape and " build " of hides is also of considerable importance regarding both personal comfort and the ability to be able to " swing " on to birds approaching at a variety of angles. Some sort of semi-roof is required at times, as I have shown later on, but whatever form the construction takes, it is quite unnecessary to crouch in a hide where the limbs become cramped and where the free use of the gun is limited. If precautions are taken to use proper materials, so that the hide " sinks " into the surrounding landscape as viewed by flying birds, its size, within reason, should not be against it, though it is absolutely essential that no movement, either of the shooter or his dog, should be seen by sharp eyes. Once the birds realise that a certain " point " in their flight-line is " occupied," they will not only avoid it, but will cleverly indicate the fact, by their behaviour in the air, to oncoming pigeon that have not so far recognised the danger, or are, as yet, too far away to have discovered it for themselves.

CHAPTER TWELVE

Pigeon Shooting—2

*" Hedge-creeping " and Stalking—Flighting—In the
Harvest Field—Shooting over Decoys—When Pigeon
come in to Roost—Organised Pigeon " Drives."*

METHODS of coming upon terms with pigeon are
numerous and most of them are open to the rough
shooter. Accordingly, I shall venture to explain the ways
best adopted for the more distinct types of shooting.

By the middle of July, if not before, the earliest hatches of
young pigeon are on wing, while many of the old birds still
appear to be in the moulting stage. Young pigeon, from
their lack of experience of the outside world, remain in-
cautious. They will sit in trees until one is well within range,
or will fly over a sportsman whose presence would be noticed
and hurriedly avoided by older birds. Adult pigeon, recovering from the moulting stage, may still have full wing-feathers
to grow and may flap out of the trees with much labour and
noise. This actually applies more to the months of April,
May and June, but during August and early September, I have
shot birds in moult that appeared to have weathered a barrage
of shots—but only just ! Hen birds shot at this time of year
are usually in poor condition, having been sitting on eggs
and then spending much time and energy on the feeding of
nestlings. Squabs (nestlings) taken from the nest just before
they have attained the inclination to fly, make excellent
eating, and many a squab-pie have I enjoyed after either

climbing trees to the nests, or poking the youngsters from the flimsy platform that constitutes their nest.

One learns that young pigeon at this stage used to be tied by a thread to one leg until they were plump enough for a pie, but such precautions seem unnecessary. In the days when live young pigeon were used as tethered decoys (this now being illegal) we used to watch certain nests and then collect the young just before they were likely to leave it. Peas and corn, soaked overnight, were used as food, the peas and grain being forced and worked down their throats, or the youngsters would take such food from the human mouth, searching for it with their broad, soft bills—greedily devouring this artificial form of " pigeon's milk." The latter in reality, of course, is the milky fluid regurgitated from the old bird's bill.

The nestling pigeon has sparse yellow down and its upper mandible is soft and broad. This latter feature remains for many months, but gradually the soft broad upper " beak " hardens and narrows, but for some time may be used to identify approximately old and young pigeon—this and the " breaking strain " of the lower mandible.

In July, then, the sportsman may wander beside tall hedgerows and belts of trees, keeping close under their shadow and shoot old or young pigeon as they make a hurried departure from their perches. He may also watch them settling in certain trees along fences, or in woodland and proceed to stalk them, always remembering that pigeon have an acute sense of hearing as well as of sight. The careless stepping on a brittle twig may cause the bird suspiciously to turn an eye in the direction of the sound and our stalker must then " freeze " until suspicion has been allayed. Old birds, morning and evening, may rest in trees, coo-ing to each other. This sound is a useful guide to the stalker, but should the coo-ing cease on the wrong note, he must immediately " freeze," for it is then obvious that the pigeon's suspicions have for some reason been roused.

PIGEON SHOOTING

From August onwards, pigeon begin to flight with definite regularity and harvest operations have commenced. Early cut corn is certain to attract pigeon, but they will also find good feeding on " laid " crops—*i.e.* wheat, etc., that has been beaten down by gales and heavy storms. I have shot pigeon at the end of July that have had their crops crammed with wheat, although the grain, to the casual eye, did not appear to be sufficiently ripe to attract rooks and pigeon. Where corn is so laid, and is being attacked by these birds, farmers are usually only too glad to invite some one to keep them off, and for this object, as also for that of good shooting, a hide must be built within range of the trouble. If some form of cover, a hedge or trees, are sufficiently close to the damage, the building of a rough hide should not be difficult, but it is necessary sometimes, and without damage to standing corn, to form a rough shelter either by propping up the laid corn, or by introducing some artificial material, such as a hurdle or two, and a few boughs, that do not show up conspicuously. A few decoys are naturally a good draw on such occasions, but some farmers will show an almost violent objection to these, holding, rightly or wrongly, that decoys tend to attract pigeon, whereas that is the last thing they desire under the circumstances. Nevertheless, the rough shooter who rents the game rights, or the keeper who is looking after the shooting interests of the ground, should do his best to keep rooks and pigeon off laid crops, thereby doing the farmer a good turn—a good turn that may be repaid, perhaps with interest, in other ways.

One golden rule, however, must be observed. On no account must the sportsman trample about in the corn, either to reach a well-laid spot, or to recover shot birds. There is usually some spot near the edge of the field where the crop is laid and I think that if birds are regularly coming to the field, a decoy may reasonably be used to draw them to this spot. From a hide against the hedge, or in the ditch pigeon may be shot and dropped outside the crop and so collected. However strong the temptation may be to gather a bird, or birds, fallen in the standing corn, this must be overcome, for in the eyes of the farmer (as it should be in the eyes of the sportsman) it is a crime either to enter standing crops, or to allow a dog to do so.

Of all the forms of pigeon shooting for sport, as being opposed to the sole object of shooting for the protection of crops, or with the object of making " record " bags, flight shooting must be considered first. Flighting pigeon, labouring against the wind, may stream over low and prove easy marks, but, coming with the wind, they will flash over the shooter as though forty dozen devils were at their tails. Again, on calm days, they will fly along their line of flight at an altitude that may or may not be within gunshot. Then it is that those birds that are in range are deceiving in pace and even a good shot may miss them again and again, shooting in front of them rather than behind them. In this respect, I have seen a poor shot, with little experience of shooting on wing, kill more pigeon than a moderately good shot, simply because he was giving the birds less " lead." On the following day, when pigeon were flighting with the wind in their tails, the man who had killed most on the previous day was shooting feet, perhaps yards, behind the mark, while his rival, still a little sore from his experience of the day before, was catching his birds in the head and crop and crumpling them with an ease that betrayed his error of yesterday. A really experienced pigeon shot would, of course, understand this change of conditions, giving his birds a good forward " lead " as they came downwind, a much lesser " lead " as they passed overhead high, but comparatively slowly, and would have taken those labouring birds, battling against the wind, well in front, " aiming " only an inch or two beyond their crops with the first barrel and choosing an easy crossing or going-away shot with the second barrel.

The actual flight-line of pigeon may be ascertained in this way. The birds may be feeding mainly in two fields at some distance apart. As they fly, a little restlessly, from one to the other, they will cross at some point, probably this point being registered as a certain tree, or clump of trees. Or they may have a direct flight line over a certain portion of fence. Again, shooting in the evening, the flight line will lie between the chosen feeding-ground and the place of roost. Perhaps there is a pond, or drinking-place on lake, or river to which they periodically flight while feeding on laid or shocked corn, or on, say, clover or turnip-tops. Anywhere, in fact, that is chosen as a regular line of flight, whether that line lasts for a day, or for a week, or is more or less general. This line must be watched and studied and a hide constructed along it, at a suitable point. Here is the spot to enjoy some first-rate shooting.

If a hide is built under trees, there is, naturally, a limited " sky-line " to cover, overhanging boughs causing a " blind " area where shots cannot be taken. The best place to build a hide, therefore, is beside a low or thin hedge over which the birds will pass. A hide of this kind may be formed with a framework of sheep hurdles, through which boughs and twigs are threaded, or of branches, their ends sharpened, stuck into the ground in a half-circle against the hedge. Again, I would emphasise that such branches must be renewed, so that they tone in with the background. There must be plenty of room in which a gun may be swung to deal with birds coming at all directions and angles, and some sort of semi-roof can be formed by a bough or two laid across the top of the hide, but not in a manner to interfere with gun-swing. If the hide is built under, or close to trees in which pigeon are expected to settle, then a little more attention will naturally be paid to " roofing." There should also be some comparatively simple form of exit, so that the shooter may hurriedly leave the hide, to gather dead birds and to retrieve

their feathers.   Loose feathers blowing about may scare
pigeon that are not too particular where they settle, but
hungry birds, perhaps feeding on kale or turnip-tops in hard
weather, will not bother much about these signs of distress,
and I have even known them attracted by them, for the
reaction of senses of semi-starved pigeon cannot be compared
with those of birds well fed, harassed and keenly suspicious.

Where the flight-line of pigeon takes them over a copse,
or a belt of trees, excellent shooting can be enjoyed, particularly if the trees are tall.   Friends of mine once built a
platform on a high tree in a wood over which pigeon flighted,
and very good sport they had after ascending the ladder and
reaching their tree-top " hide."   I doubt, however, except in
special circumstances, whether the trouble of going to this
extent is really worth while, for pigeon must enter and leave
a wood, and ambushed at such points may afford good shooting as they fly in or out, or circle lower and lower before
dropping into the trees.

The shooting of pigeon in the harvest field may prove
easy, or results can be definitely disappointing.   Where
harvesting operations are general, the birds have an enormous
area over which to feed and consequently may leave one spot
from which they have been shot, for another.   At the same
time, the judicious use of decoys have always the chance, and
the good chance, of attracting passing birds.   And it must be
added that pigeon are continuously on the move when disturbed by harvesters shocking the sheaves, or carting them
from the field.   Once I find a spot favoured by pigeon, I like
to reach it at daybreak, before the birds have left their roost,
and there form a hide of sheaves and place a set of decoys in
natural feeding attitudes about the shocks within shooting
distance.   Presently, a few pigeon will arrive, circle lazily
on seeing the decoys and descend to join them.   The first
sounds of shooting will disturb other pigeon within hearing
from their roosts and soon there will be birds flying to and

fro, settling on the corn and every now and again rising to seek a fresh pitch, seemingly afraid that they are missing better feeding in another portion of the field. Without decoys, a little shooting might be done, but at this time of year young pigeon are plentiful and the sight of decoys is hard to resist, even though shots are being fired every few minutes. Dead birds should be gathered every now and again, when a lull in the " battle " allows and a few may be placed in life-like attitudes about the shocks, to add to the reality of the scene.

Pigeon feed mainly twice a day—in the morning and evening, or, as the days draw in, during the afternoon. First thing in the morning the birds will set out for the fields, but many will remain in the trees to sun and continue their slumbers. These will later join the " early birds " and by about nine or ten o'clock, all the pigeon will have left their roosts and will be busy earning a living. By noon, those that have filled their crops will be found taking a short siesta, but will fly out to the feeding-grounds again during the afternoon.

Shooting over decoys is an art, the greater benefits of which come with experience. There are several types of decoy, and I do not consider that, once the game is understood, there is much to choose between them, except with reference to simplified transport. The old wooden type of carved and painted decoy can be made to look sufficiently realistic to act as a draw, but its weight and bulk are against it, for to attempt to carry half a dozen to a dozen of these would be a hard day's work in itself, if the shooting-ground was far from home. The light canvas-shell types of decoy are definitely the best and most convenient to use, for they fit into one another and several may thus be carried in the game bag, or even the hare-pocket. Arranged in a life-like group on their steel-needle supports, and with their heads to the wind, they look from the ground, or from above, extraordinarily natural and the slight movement which the wind may cause, adds to the reality of the scene. They appear, of course, more natural when grouped on the ground than on sheaves of corn, but even on the latter they have excellent drawing power and young pigeon in particular come freely to them.

I think, however, that every keen pigeon shooter should be in possession of one or more stuffed pigeon, for nothing more natural could be made and, though, here again, bulk may be against the carrying of several of them, one or more placed on the sheaves of corn, or a little way off from a group of canvas decoys, prove an additional aid to successful decoying.

There is, too, the mechanical decoy—a natural enough bird and one which opens and shuts its wings when a button is pressed in the hide. A length of flex wire runs between the decoy and the hide and the movement is supplied by electric current. Now, the value of such a decoy lies in its ability to attract the eyes of passing and even distant birds through the movement of its wings. Any one who has done much shooting from a hide over decoys realises that " still " decoys are often overlooked, or ignored by pigeon flying past at a distance, whether they be single birds, small groups or large flocks. But press the button of your mechanical decoy at the psychological moment and the quick flapping of wings is almost certain to catch the eyes of passing birds which will then, as likely as not, turn to investigate, when another press of the button will further result in intriguing them. Such movement, however, must not be overdone. I have shot over home-made mechanical decoys and have been much impressed by the way they have attracted pigeon that would otherwise have passed on.

There are other types of decoys and gadgets which have definite drawing powers and consequently may be considered as worthy additions to the equipment of the sportsman who thoroughly appreciates the sport of pigeon shooting in its various forms. There are telescopic rods on which decoy pigeons may be lifted to the tree-top, there to attract others. There is also a type of sling that casts a weight over a high branch, when a decoy may be pulled up to a sitting position overhead. There are certain dead trees or boughs which pigeon greatly favour when the leaves are still on the trees. They use these as look-out posts, and feel themselves safe from attack. Decoys used on these bare outposts will be found to draw both pigeon and doves, when, from his hide at the foot of the tree, or in a ditch or fence within range, the shooter can get some excellent sport at incoming birds. And I may add that a head-on shot at doves that have been much disturbed by shooting and are therefore suspicious and fly at considerable speed, is a shot that will defeat even the most confident shot far more times than he will care to remember. To kill, then, with your second barrel a pigeon or dove out of a small lot, or a flock that has " detonated," is a feat the satisfaction of which comes as a just reward.

A whole book might be written on the detailed technique of shooting over decoys, but the elementary principles concerned are to find a spot where pigeon are feeding in numbers, construct a satisfactory hide and arrange your decoys in a natural group and in natural positions. You may decoy pigeon almost anywhere, but only big bags will be shot when the spot chosen is much favoured by the birds, it being attractive on account of its feeding value. A decoy or two placed at a pond, or, say, on the grass of a river meadow will certainly draw a few birds, but the chances offered to the shooter cannot be compared with those open to him on planted land, or on crops to which it is seen pigeon are flocking at feeding time.

Although I have made many big bags over decoys, I have made even bigger ones when shooting pigeon coming in to roost at night. I have perhaps been favoured by doing most of my pigeon shooting in a neighbourhood where there are a number of small fir coverts and belts of trees into which pigeon literally swarm during the late autumn and winter months. All about the distant hills are big beech-woods and to these the pigeon, particularly the immense " foreign " droves, come when the beech masts are ripe. Local pigeon shooters take advantage of the influx to enjoy a week or two's shooting, and it is then that tens of thousands of pigeon leave the big woods with bulging crops and descend into the sheltered valleys with their tree-belts and fir woods to roost. Should a storm sweep the hills, the pigeon race in before it, and I have many times shot and shot, until the barrels of the gun were too hot to hold, at birds hurtling into shelter before a driving hailstorm.

It was on one such evening, when I had taken a good supply of cartridges with me to enjoy this form of shooting, that a terrific thunderstorm burst over the hills and hailstones swept the countryside, almost blotting out the form of trees a field away. Sheltering behind a tree on the edge of a long, narrow wood, I shot bird after bird as the pigeon raced in low before the storm. By the time I had run out of cart-ridges, I had accounted for well over a hundred pigeon and a friend had shot over eighty. As we stood there, with not a cartridge between us, the pigeon continued to pour into the wood until it seemed every tree and bush was occupied by a few, or many, birds. While we still had cartridges left we had shot birds on wing as they arrived, but between the times of their coming, we turned and knocked sitting pigeon from the trees. Nor did others take much notice of the din of battle ; they flew up as we fired, but in a minute were settled again, almost stunned, it seemed, by the force of the gale and the blinding rain and hailstones.

On other evenings I have sat in a fir covert where the trees were from fifteen to twenty feet high and shot pigeon with a ·410 as they crossed between gaps in the tree-tops. With the evening sun playing over the rolling downlands, I have chosen an open spot among the firs on a steep hillside and from my vantage point watched pigeon approaching from their feeding-grounds and enjoyed good shooting as they arrived overhead.

Yet, whatever type of country, whatever kind of wood attracts pigeon to roost in numbers, it is always advisable to have one or more friends stationed at strategic points, to keep the birds on the move. When pigeon are fired at from one end of a covert, they will invariably make for the other. That is, if the covert is of some size and the birds are reluctant to leave it for fresh quarters. In my opinion, the ideal wood is a long narrow one, the length of which will be flown by pigeon disturbed by shooting. By the time they have reached the far end the shock will have worn off and, after circling once or twice, one or two venturesome spirits will drop down, followed by the entire flock. Further shooting, and the birds will seek sanctuary at the end of the wood from which they recently arrived, by this time having forgotten the hot reception they received there.

It is this type of pigeon shooting round which big " county " pigeon drives are organised. Farmers, keepers and those invited by them arrange to meet on a number of specified nights (perhaps once a week, or once a fortnight) and man the surrounding woods and belts where pigeon are known to roost. Perhaps there is a hundred-acre wood, and in this, at vantage points, ten or more guns may be stationed. In larger woods, it is often arranged for one gun to hold a roving commission. That is, he is given the job of keeping birds on the move, by firing at those that have settled in large numbers and where no gun is stationed. Immense bags of pigeon have been recorded at these organised drives, particularly in Yorkshire.

Granted that the organisation is good, which, alas, it often is not, the drawback to these shoots lies in the inexperience of a large number of the guns present. Anxious to show a good individual bag and quite failing to appreciate the maximum range of the modern shotgun, pigeon are shot at when far too high, with the result that, instead of circling lower with the object of settling, the flocks immediately take fright and make off elsewhere, all too often to meet with the same foolish reception. Eventually, of course, they clear off to woods outside the limit of the organisation. Flocks seen to be circling and obviously considering settling, should be left well alone, either until they have actually come down on to the trees and undergrowth, or until they are well within range. If they are allowed to do this, it will give other guns stationed near the opportunity to get some shooting as the startled birds scatter. The gun who neglects to understand these points not only returns with few, if any, pigeon to show for a great number of cartridges expended, but he will earn the unpopularity he deserves for spoiling the sport of others.

Always remember, on these occasions, to have patience, to consider others taking part in the shoot and to retain, in the excitement of the moment, at least a semblance of knowledge of the powers of your weapon. Hasty and wild shooting, with little thought as to killing range, will not only spoil your own chances of bringing in a respectable bag, but must ruin the chances of neighbouring guns. Many excellent and enthusiastic pigeon shooters of my acquaintance have given up attending these useful pigeon drives, simply because, their patience sorely tried, they refuse to shoot in the company of those who have neither learned, nor will ever allow themselves to learn, that self-control is essential to every branch of shooting, especially that in which the sport of others is at stake.

CHAPTER THIRTEEN

Rough Shooting

What is " Rough Shooting " ?—The Amateur Keeper
—Pheasants, Partridges and Duck—Making a Warren
—Patience and Perseverance.

"ROUGH Shooting to Let " is an advertisement we often see in our papers, but when one asks oneself " What is the definition of ' rough shooting ' ? " it will be found that the answer covers a wide range of possibilities. In Ireland, for instance, it is possible to take a rough shoot of many thousands of acres almost " for a song," while there is no reason why a man who has the shooting over 50 acres of game-productive ground should not consider himself the tenant of a small rough shoot. Broadly speaking, I would define any shooting as rough shooting where game is not artificially reared or systematically driven and where no keeper is employed. In short, where sport is not organised. Thus, in my estimation, a farm or farms over which one rents the shooting and where one walks round when the spirit moves one, may be termed a rough shoot, whereas if a sportsman, or a syndicate of sportsmen takes it and, though not employing a proper keeper, shoot over it as a party, walking-up or driving birds on specified dates, then the term " rough shooting " no longer applies.

Some years ago, I took for £2 the shooting rights over 48 acres of water-meadows beside a river. In one season—when, admittedly, we experienced an unusually hard winter—I shot on this small piece of ground 21 brace of partridges,

31 pheasants, over 300 snipe (when snipe were on the move day and night, seeking out open springs and other feeding-grounds in a frozen world, I visited this shoot often three times a day, to find quantities of snipe there on almost every occasion), 38 hares, 6 rabbits, countless pigeon and a number of duck, including five different species. So although 48 acres is only a small bit of ground, when it produces game and various to this, or lesser extent, it is entitled to be called a " rough shoot."

Not long ago I received a letter from a stranger asking for my advice on his 5-acre shoot on which he had killed an excellent and varied bag the year before, including geese, duck and curlew. Fortunately, my feelings were relieved next day when I received a second letter from him saying that through a slip of the typewriter he had missed out an o and that his shoot comprised 50 acres !

On very large rough shoots, the sportsman will kill a good deal of vermin, but he has not the same opportunity of keeping it almost completely in check as he c n do on a smaller place. On a shoot of under 200 acres, traps can be kept set at every vantage point, while the stock of partridges is known and the whereabouts and numerical strength of every covey can be continually checked. When coveys split up into pairs, note will be taken of the ground occupied by these pairs, and it will then be a comparatively simple matter to discover their nests, and to protect those that are inclined to be " open " to the sharp eyes of winged vermin. A few strands of briar drawn across the entrance run to this nest, a branch pulled into position over that one, may, without disturbing the sitting bird, help to conceal eggs which might, being sat on and accordingly highly polished, attract undesirable attention.

That is the advantage of a shoot which one man can look after in his spare time and also improve so that vermin is reduced to a minimum while game increases. Apart from trapping and shooting vermin and keeping an eye on nests, there are many ways of improving a small shoot. To be on good terms with the land tenant and his men is essential. And a couple of rabbits, or pigeon given to a farm labourer may result in his reporting nests he has found, or vermin he has seen. Mutual regard leads to mutual benefit. For instance, when a hedge is being laid, or trimmed, if the trimmings, instead of being burned are laid along the bottom of the hedge, they will keep cattle and horses from nibbling growing shoots, and, grass and other vegetation growing up through them, first-rate and attractive shelter is formed for partridge nests. If, on the other hand, hedges have already been trimmed and the trimmings are lying in heaps ready for burning, a friendly farmer, if approached, will order them to be burned before pheasants and partridges choose them as nesting sites. I have seen hedge-trimmings burnt although it was known that partridges were nesting among them, or, if it was not realised by the farmer, it could have been pointed out to him with good advantage by the shooting tenant. Likewise, it is a habit with some farmers to burn the coarse grass along banks and on the sides of ditches during dry weather, and at a time when game is nesting— a job that could well be done in March or early April, or left until June or July.

If there is a small pond about the rough shoot, in the open, or in a covert, it is good fun, if time can be spared, to rear a few duck. The eggs of a known flying strain can be procured from a game farm, hatched under a hen and, when a few weeks old, the young duck can be taken in coops to the vicinity of the pond and can be weaned off meal on to a corn diet, when a handful or two a day thrown to them regularly, or scattered in shallow water where small birds are unable to get it, will keep them at home. Thus a pleasant addition to the game book may be made at very little cost, but it is essential to keep down vermin in the vicinity, especially rats which have an uncanny way of discovering young duck and will run great risks to get at them.

If pheasants are reared on the next shoot, it is not sportsman-like to attempt to attract them over the border by hand-feeding, but that is not to say that the normal feeding of one's own birds, which, incidentally of course, may "draw" a few outside birds, need be neglected. Indeed, at harvest time the farmer should be approached and a load of rakings, preferably from a field of barley, be procured from him if there are any coverts on the shoot. These rakings should then be built up on a low platform of poles into what are known as feed-stacks; that is to say, miniature stacks of from 6 to 9 ft. square. The object of these stacks, placed at vantage points about a wood is to keep pheasants on the shoot from roaming. Every now and again a few handfuls of rakings can be drawn from the stacks and scattered on the ground, forming scratching places on which the birds will converge to scratch for odd grains of corn. A few handfuls of grain occasionally thrown into the litter on the ground will be welcomed by pheasants, which quickly find such spots and visit them daily. The object of the platforms is to prevent ground vermin from ambushing feeding birds and also to stop rabbits from "working" the stacks. These platforms must be built sufficiently high to prevent foxes from crouching unseen under them.

The feeding of partridges is not necessary, except in hard weather, when a little wheat and dari seed, or weed seeds left over when corn is threshed, can be scattered in the places where coveys are known to feed or jug (jug, or juk, being a term used for roosting on the ground). A little feed in hard weather or during late autumn, winter and early spring, helps to keep up the stamina of the birds and so checks disease, and the spots chosen for it should be away from the direct vicinity of trees and hedges infested by small birds.

Rabbits must always form an interesting side to a rough

shoot, and, if there are none on the ground, it is a comparatively simple matter to introduce a few. With this object in mind, cart a few loads of thorns or build a small faggot-pile in the centre of the shoot, and where rabbits are unlikely to do damage. The best site is a fence or bank into which rabbits will burrow, for there is not much sport to be obtained at burrows in open, flat ground. Wire-netting sufficiently high to prevent rabbits jumping over should be dug, or ploughed in to a fair depth (to prevent burrowing underneath) round the pile and far enough out from it to allow rabbits to feed. Now obtain four doe rabbits and a buck, or six does and two bucks and release them in the enclosure. A few roots thrown in and a little hay, etc., will help to feed them, if there is insufficient natural matter, and they will quickly dig themselves in. Once good-sized burrows have been formed, the wire-netting can be removed, and by the following season there will be found the nucleus of a stock of rabbits—a nucleus from which a few rabbits may be obtained for the larder. Needless to say, traps must be set along hedgerows in the vicinity of this experiment while the wire-netting remains in place, or stoats and weasels will take an interest in it, while poaching cats must not be tolerated.

Visiting the site of an experiment of this kind one day, I saw, to my horror, a black cat disappear into my faggot-pile. Taking council with myself, I decided, after some meditation, to enter a big line-ferret, which I muzzled with string. As the burrows were small, the cat bolted almost immediately and I saw to it that I held the gun steady. I do not know how long this cat had been at large, but I discovered the remains of a half-grown rabbit, with the skin rolled back, partly buried a few yards from a hole—certain evidence that Moggins had already been busy!

Rough shoots, particularly if they are small, benefit greatly by being kept quiet. Continual shooting and disturbance not only makes game wild and inclined to seek out quieter ground, but welcome visitors, like snipe and duck, will never regard as a new-found sanctuary ground on which they cannot feed or rest in peace. If duck show an inclination to visit ponds and ditches about the place, a little regular feeding with corn helps to attract them, and rotten potatoes and apples cast into shallow water is an incentive to them to pay the spot a visit by night, and, if not unduly harassed, they will remain there by day.

I know how very tempting it is, when keepering a small shoot of this kind, to shoot game and various whenever the chance occurs. Sometimes, it is true, if opportunity is not taken, the chance may not again present itself. But there are fair-sized rough shoots on which over-shooting can do far more harm than good, and it is splendid training for the young shot sometimes to resist temptation and sanely to consider the future and his original determination to build up a rough shoot that will be a credit to his perseverance and presently offer him the best of sport.

CHAPTER FOURTEEN

The Grouse

*Moorland Impressions—Nesting Habits—Migration—
Driving—Shooting over Dogs—Black Game—Capercaillie—Ptarmigan.*

IN one respect, the red grouse is outstanding—he is the only game-bird that is unique to the British Isles. Familiar to those who are fortunate enough to visit the moors at different times of the year, he is, nevertheless, a " strange " bird to those who know him only as a corpse suspended from a hook in the poulterer's shop. The grouse is generally distributed throughout Scotland and Wales, and in England as far south as Shropshire, Derbyshire and Yorkshire. Certain experiments at introducing it even farther south have not been altogether unsuccessful, as those well acquainted with certain parts of the south-west country are probably aware.

My first introduction to the grouse took place many years ago on the Derbyshire moors. I still remember how impressed I was with the general rugged atmosphere round the Peak District, the sweep of the purple-clad undulating moors, the stone-walls and the mountain sheep that jumped them as our car passed, but particularly with an old cock grouse that sat in a stunted thorn by the roadside, his very attitude a challenge to our right to share with him the freedom of the hills. As we drew slowly level with him, the sun shone on his rich plumage and red wattle, but as the car pulled up within a few yards, his courage seemed visibly to shrink, and with a rapid " kok ! kok ! kok ! " the stout, short-winged bird flew off over the heather from the safe cover of which he implored us to " go-back ! go-back ! go-back ! "

The chief charm of grouse shooting undoubtedly lies in the strange, fresh and impressive environment in which one finds oneself on journeying north from the flat farmlands of southern England. Somehow, as one walks knee-deep in the heather, with a vista of colourful moorland spreading away in front to the dim outline of hills, one gets the feeling that one is on the roof of the world where the air is fresh and clear and where Nature walks unspoiled above the heads of men and all the soot and grime and stench of modern life. Here, where all is quiet, except for the far-distant voices of a shepherd and his sheep and the occasional challenge of a grouse, or the shrill piping of a lonely pipit, a fresh field of thought and action is opened to the young sportsman whose first visit it is to the land of grouse and heather.

Far, far away seem the rabbit-haunted hedgerows, the pale yellow stubble of the barley fields where the coveys are calling, the shady woodland rides across which the pheasants scamper. And yet, in this world of change, there are many ties which bind one to the lore of southern farmlands. In many respects, the grouse is similar to the partridge, and if a covey of grouse came suddenly over a tall whitethorn hedge, detonating as do partridges, on seeing the waiting guns, I have no doubt that the young sportsman, keeping his head, would not find in this larger bird with proportionately shorter wings a more difficult shot. Indeed, were it not that grouse so often fly low, the natural colour of their plumage fitting in so well with the colours of the moor, thus making somewhat deceptive their distance and the speed of their flight, I would say that they were far easier to kill than the little grey birds of the roots and cornfields hurtling suddenly into sight over the top of the hedge.

Perhaps the strongest link that binds the northern moors

with southern arables is to be found on the fringe of the heather, where grouse occasionally raid the harvest fields, and where a few coveys of partridges may be flushed from the moor. Here grouse and partridges may be shot on common land.

The grouse nests in April, laying an average clutch of from 7 to 10 richly coloured yellowish eggs closely blotched with reddish brown. Although not perhaps quite such devoted parents as partridges, grouse are, nevertheless, much concerned with the well-being of their young and prepared to do battle with any vermin which takes an unhealthy interest in the family.

Early in the season, after a few days of shooting, the coveys often pack, but the immense packs that one sees later on during the season, particularly in hard weather, are probably formed as the result of migratory instinct. Grouse will leave a moor for several reasons—lack of food, or water, or on account of really bad weather. During a blizzard pack after pack may be seen leaving higher ground for lower moors, and sometimes a keeper will wake to find his moor " alive " with grouse where but yesterday there were few, while elsewhere, you may be certain, there is another keeper mourning a loss !

There is still a lot to be learned concerning the migration of grouse, and at present the problems are the subject of an inquiry, while experiments in ringing young grouse, in order to discover their movements, have continued for some seasons. The food of the grouse is varied, for it consumes among a host of other things, heather shoots, crowberry, blaeberry, cranberry, cotton sedge, sheep's sorrel, bog myrtle and shoots, seeds and leaves of various vegetation. The young feed largely on insects and caterpillars. During the heat of the day grouse lie up in the shelter of tall heather and ling, or in the shadow of the shoulder of a hill. Morning and evening, or during a cool day, you will find them in the vicinity of burns, seeking the grit which is essential to their health. This they also find beside roads, where the passer-by will often see them dusting while basking in the sunshine.

On most moors driving grouse is now the rule, although in the north of Scotland and in Ireland there are still a number of moors where grouse are shot over dogs before driving starts. The young shot, if he applies the principles I have laid down in the chapter on behaviour in the shooting field and, indeed, throughout this book, to the more conventional forms of shooting, he need not feel concern when invited to join a shooting party on the moors. He should have gathered how to approach his butt and how to behave when ensconced and after the drive is over.

What I feel he will concern himself with will be how to get out on to the moors with a keeper, or a companion, to shoot grouse over a trained pointer or setter, while remember-ing that on most moors there are often bits of marshy ground and stretches of water, where snipe and duck may help to add variety to the bag and where golden plover, teal and other birds with which he is not so intimately acquainted may be found.

Shooting grouse over dogs can be a real pleasure, but of late years the birds get wild earlier than they used to, and I think the reason for this may be due to driving and also, where heather is short and of a less holding nature, to systematic heather-burning.

But see! Ahead there in the heather old Shot has stopped dead and has grown as rigid as a board, one front paw lifted. It is obvious that he has got the wind of a squatting covey. Let us walk quietly up to him and en-courage him forward. Now, look out! The parent birds are first away, the remainder of the covey straggling up one by one—a late brood of cheepers. Possibly they are old enough to look after themselves, but somehow we feel that it would be wrong to shoot the old birds. And so onwards, admiring the work of steady old Shot as he quarters his ground, scenting the wind and every now and again glancing back to see if everything is correct !

To tell the difference between the sexes of grouse during the shooting season is comparatively simple, the best test being to look at the chin feathers ; in the cock these are a chestnut-red. Old birds may be told from young in various ways. There is the test which holds good with all birds— the degree of softness of the lower mandible. A surer test, however, is to examine the toes, for birds of the year do not shed their claws, while old birds may show the mark where claws have been shed, or may still retain claws ready for shedding which can be removed by gentle pulling, coming away like casing in the fingers.

Fortunate indeed is the youthful sportsman who has the opportunity to walk the moors and the high hills, particularly if accompanied by a keeper willing to impart knowledge to his pupil. Some young shots there are whose homes lie amid the moors and the mountains ; others are able to pay an annual visit to these surroundings of delight ; still others there are who must content themselves with a rare visit. Here, where the stags roar on the forests (and a stalk after stag or hind is an expedition of novel charm) ; where the golden eagle wheels on motionless wings, watching the feeding hare in the corrie far below ; where salmon rivers and small mountain burns attract the fisherman ; where on moor and moss the red grouse throws a challenge to the world and the swift-winged wildfowl gather—here, I say, is the paradise of sportsmen young and old, but a paradise, alas, which only the limited and fortunate few can enjoy.

The Black Grouse.—Black game are usually to be found in northern woodlands and on the fringes of moors and hilly country where there is a variety of feeding-ground, including cultivated land, for the blackcock and his wife, the grey hen, are very partial to a raid on the sheaves of the harvest field, while their love for the tips of conifer shoots have earned for them the ire of the Forestry Commissioners who have been directly or indirectly responsible for the destruction of many nests.

While the blackcock differs from the red grouse in his glossy blue-black plumage and lyre-shaped tail, the grey hen is a far less distinctive bird, with reddish-brown plumage. The strong flight of black game is much akin to that of grouse and a crime of the moors over which many a " fine " has been paid out, and many a young sportsman been censured is the killing of a grey hen between August 12th and August 20th, when the shooting season for black game commences. And though the grey hen is a larger bird than the red grouse (black grouse being next to the capercaillie in size) and should be fairly easily identified, " accidents will happen," and it is also to be feared that the law is not always adhered to when an old blackcock comes forward at the head of the grouse pack during the first seven days of the grouse shooting season !

Many experiments have been made to introduce black game into fresh localities, for it is a sporting bird and an asset to any rough shoot, but they have met with very little success. In Ireland there are no black game.

The most noted feature of the black grouse is the annual display of the males which takes place on early spring mornings. At a chosen spot, the birds gather, the cocks combining to " lec," as their competitive performances are called, while the hens form an audience. With hoarse cries, leaping high in the air and cutting all manner of antics, the male birds fight and dance, showing off before the grey hens and attacking rivals with a ferocity that has more bluff and bluster about it than deadly combat, although feathers do fly and sometimes serious damage accrues. These displays of courtship have so often been described in books, that it is unnecessary for me to give a word-picture of a very interesting, extravagant and amusing scene.

The Capercaillie.—This handsome bird, " Cock of the Woods " in districts of northern Scotland, will not interest the average young sportsman, except from an ornithological point of view, although a giant cock caper added to the bag of those who have the opportunity of shooting in the northern woods and forests is an " item " that will remain in memory. Most of us, however, who have not seen it in its natural haunts are content to regard it as a sort of wild turkey, which gives a display of courtship almost as strange as that of the blackcock. Having fought for the favour of the hens, the victorious bird perches on a branch or rock, spreads its ruff and tail, and, drooping its wings, produces its strange serenade. Of this " song " Coward writes, " Various observers have heard notes which reminded them of the squalls of fighting cats, of the drawing of corks and the sound of grinding knives." Apparently such wild music " goes down well " with the hens, for, gathering around their lord they view his display with unveiled admiration !

The Ptarmigan.—As with the capercaillie, only a limited number of young sportsmen get the opportunity of shooting this bird, which belongs rather to the rocky summits than to the moorland. It has, I am told, a swift flight, but, like the red-legged partridge, prefers to use its legs rather than its wings, but when in the air it will cross valleys at a great height as it flies from peak to peak. It occurs only in the highest mountains of Scotland where it is the natural quarry of the hill-fox and the golden eagle, although its grey and white plumage tones in well with the snow and the stones among which it lives. " Ptarmigan " you may see advertised in many shops, but were those who sell the very great majority of them strictly truthful, they would label the birds " Imported Willow Grouse " !

CHAPTER FIFTEEN

The Pheasant

Characteristics—The Rearing-field—On the "Feed"
—Covert Shooting—Hedge-hunting—Appreciation.

THE pheasant may be described as a long-established
alien, the introduction of which is lost in antiquity!
Various pheasants have been brought to this country and
have interbred with older stock, so that to-day it might be
said with truth that the original pheasant has no existence,
although its characteristics are observed in the "species"
we see in the woodlands and about the fields. The old
English ring-necked appears to be the Britisher of the various
kinds, including the Chinese, the Mongolian and the
Melanistic Mutant, which latter is a "sport" and is better
known as the black pheasant.

While it is generally accepted that pheasants roost in
trees, I doubt if this habit is natural with them, for this
reason. The pheasant is a bird of the eastern swamps, and
its likeness for low, damp ground is obvious, for marshes
and willow-beds always seem to attract it, and in the former
you will find plenty of evidence that it prefers to juk among
the reeds and coarse grass, evidence, in fact, that is not
lacking even in the water-logged meadows in the vicinity of
coverts.

On one pheasant shoot in which I was interested, we had
considerable trouble in getting the birds up to roost, although
the coverts were composed of larch and Scotch firs with a
fringe of elms. Many evenings in the year were spent in

flushing pheasants, as dusk approached, from the thick grass of hillsides and from the cover of scrub, and gently persuadir g them to seek the safer shelter of the trees. It was necessary to take these precautions, as foxes were plentiful.

At times one reads about the damage to crops by pheasants, but when this does occur to any extent it is where pheasants are reared in large numbers and find their way to the sheaves of the harvest field, or on to newly planted ground before the keeper realises their intentions. It is obvious that he would not allow them to cause damage of this kind if he could help it, for he would not welcome the complaints or actions of farmers with whom he prefers to be on the most friendly terms. While it is true that pheasants will eat considerable quantities of grain, they are also great devourers of wire-worms and other injurious insects, and their love for the spangle gall of the oak and for acorns is well known. In fact, the rough shooter may consider himself fortunate if there are a few oak trees along the hedgerows of his shoot, or in his coverts, for, in due season, pheasants will be found in their vicinity.

In the chapter on partridges I have said that the pheasant is a bad mother, but she is also a careless bird, sometimes dropping eggs in strange places and seemingly forgetting all about them. It is no strange thing to discover the eggs of a pheasant in a partridge nest, or in that of a mallard, but occasionally she will resort to higher places and use the old nest of a pigeon or a crow high up in a tree. One can only suppose that the young when born, as do those of the mallard (which not infrequently chooses to nest in a tree) fall from the nest, and by their very lightness almost float down to earth. At any rate, they land without injury.

The pheasant lays from ten to fifteen eggs, though eleven might be the average, but will produce forty or more if penned for laying and her eggs removed as laid. On a pheasant shoot, the birds are fed to keep them at home and, when it is desired to pick them up for the laying pen, food is scattered under home-made " cages " and those which are healthy and show no signs of having been " pricked " by stray pellets are released in the pen. Once sufficient eggs have been laid and gathered for rearing purposes, the birds are released, and go away, often to lay a small clutch on their own and bring up a family.

A description of the rearing of pheasants on a large scale will not interest the average young shot, but I would most earnestly advise him to get in touch with a keeper who will allow him to see how the eggs are hatched off under hens and the broods on the rearing-field. I cannot imagine the youthful sportsman who would be anything but thrilled in the process, for no more intimate knowledge of game preservation can be obtained than that which surrounds the rearing-field with its lines and lines of coops and its scores of broods. Here, on the sunlit hillside, the keeper goes the rounds of his charges, feeding and watering them, while keeping a weather eye open for attacks by vermin.

As a youth, and since, I have spent many long but indescribably pleasant hours sitting in one corner of a bird-field, as it is often called, waiting for rooks, jackdaws and hawks to swoop down on the tiny chicks busy in the long grass round the coops. Incidentally, on the bird-field, coops should face in various directions, so that the old hen foster-mothers can view the sky all round, or the hens should be tethered to a spar of the coop by a short cord. It is surprising how quickly even the domestic hen spies a spot in the sky and immediately recognises it as an enemy. Keen and alert though the watchman may be, he will often be put on his guard by the warning " growl " of an old hen and he will see by her actions from which direction danger is advancing.

And what a sight is the pheasant " feed " in covert, when the keeper whistles and feeds his flock. The tamer of the birds will immediately run out on to the ride and commence to feed, then from almost every point of cover bright eyes and bright plumage show and the " feed " begins to fill with hungry birds. Now a couple of moorhen join the throng and the keeper mumbles threats, for he cannot afford to feed such greedy birds, if he is to keep his accounts down. Now flocks of greenfinches, sparrows and chaffinches descend from every angle to hop about among the 200 pheasants present. Let a stranger appear suddenly and the effect is startling. In a moment the ride will be empty and only glimpses of anxious pheasants will be had among the undergrowth.

And so it is when the shooting season commences. We read a great deal about hand-reared pheasants being as fat and tame as barndoor fowl and what a crime it is to shoot them. Yet the pheasants we are watching in the " feed " from the shelter of the keeper's hut will be as wild as their wild brothers and sisters as the beaters fall into line among the trees and commence their tapping. Then, with the speed of deer, the birds will leg it " forrard," presently to crash upwards through the roof of the wood, the old cocks calling a challenge to the guns standing in the valley below. A rocketing pheasant is a shot for the expert, and many an amateur has reason to believe that if the pheasant had a tail a yard long he would still shoot underneath it ! Where pheasants are driven from one covert to another over flat land, there is not a great deal of skill required to floor them, but, sent streaming over a valley, with the guns over 100 ft. below the highest, and with a cross-wind that makes the birds curl, then pheasant shooting becomes a real test of skill.

The young sportsman, however, will be more concerned with the pheasants of the rough shoot, and I am quite sure that they will give him just as much sport as they offer the gun who has them driven over him. The pheasant prefers to use its legs as much as possible and to rise on wing only when hard pressed. Thus, when hunting out hedgerows, patches of kale, or roots, the sportsman must be prepared for the pheasant he watched enter cover at one spot to rise from another well out of range, if a dog is in pursuit. When hedge-hunting, and ditches are dry, if two guns are working together, they should not walk one each side of the fence, but one should stand well forward at the end or junction of the hedge, while the other attempts to keep up with the questing dog. Then those pheasants which leg it down the fence will be taken by surprise, whereas, if the guns had kept together, they, the pheasants, would have run down the ditch and risen with a chortle far out of range.

When the shooter and his dog are on their own, the former should keep ahead of his dog if it is on the line of a pheasant, for once the bird has reached the end of the hedge it is most likely to make a break for freedom long before the dog catches up with it. Remember, pheasants on their own ground know every inch of it and their cunning is proverbial. Remember also to shoot well over a rising pheasant, for nearly all the misses at this type of shot result from shooting under the target—a target that looks larger and slower-rising than is actually the case.

Although I cannot have the same respect for the pheasant as I have for the little brown bird with the horseshoe crest, I certainly admire the gaudy strutting cock, crowing and flapping his wings in the sunlight, or displaying before his harem of admiring hens. His mind is a network of cunning and of cooler reasoning than one finds in most birds. Watch him come forward well ahead of the beaters, hesitate at the edge of the ride, listen attentively, then, suddenly making up his mind, dart back along his own tracks to lie doggo beneath a fallen bough, his bright eyes the only sign that he is a thing alive.

Watch him, hard pressed, fly quietly up into a tree and

144

Young shots following more safety principles

A joint effort—bringing home the bag

peer down at the beaters as they advance all unconscious of his presence above them !

Track him in the snow and he will tire you out, for his trail will take you along the steep hillside, threading the junipers as it goes, down to and across the floor of the valley and up the far slope. A full mile onwards and the tracks lead into a dense thicket where the snow clings to the bushes like a thick white hood and the trees stand silent as the grave. In goes the dog, and presently with a fine flurry and a loud chortle of glee up crashes our old cock, the weak sunlight playing upon his jewelled plumage. Up he comes towards us, then suddenly corkscrews back, placing a tree-trunk between himself and danger. A rather long, and I regret to say, wild shot and we watch him depart against the background of snow-covered hills and the brown smudge of larch trees, and only the disgust with which the spaniel regards us makes us laugh outright.

Was it not Mr. Patrick Chalmers who drew the curtain over such a scene, when he wrote those words long burned into my memory ? :

" Where the snow-powdered hillside rings hard to the tread,
He's not for the pick-up ;
Hark, there's his hoarse hiccup
Afar in the twilight, blue-jewelled and chill—
The splendid old blackguard who laughs at us still ! "

And was it not Mr. Eric Parker who wrote thus of the pheasant ? :

" What is the most typical sound of a winter afternoon ? The delicate little song of the hedge-sparrow ; the twitter of a flock of pied wagtails, at flight before roosting ; the chack-chack of fieldfares overhead ; the huntsman's horn—these are all true sounds of winter. But I think the prodigious clatter of a cock pheasant going up to roost has more of the essence of January in it than the others. It means sunset,

L   145

dusk, woods, a quiet sky ; such a sky as the Scholar Gypsy stood to gaze at, beyond the signal-elm on the ridge. And if that is winter, the crow of a cock pheasant in April is the spring ; can you hear it without thinking of orchids, hazel-stubs, primroses ? ''

I answer that I cannot !

CHAPTER SIXTEEN

The Partridge

The Partridge at Home—Habits of Coveys—According to Weather — Partridge Shooting — Phraseology— " Frenchmen."

MOST beloved of our game-birds is the native grey partridge, to which even the budding sportsman requires no introduction. Common to farm land, it is also distributed among upland pastureland and is to be seen on the fringes of the moors. Unfortunately, modern methods of agriculture tend to have an adverse effect on the well-being of the bird, for not only has the transition of much arable land into pasture deprived it of a great deal of its natural food and cover, but to-day the plough turns in the stubble almost as soon as harvest is over, and even where stubble remains, poultry is housed upon it in large flocks. The result is that spilled grain and seeds are consumed by poultry and pigeon droves, which, at the same time, foul the ground and are responsible in great part for some of the diseases which attack the coveys.

From the feeding point of view, the partridge is undoubtedly beneficial to agriculture. While it may eat a certain amount of spilled corn, its chief diet consists of insects, weed-seeds, grass and fresh shoots of clover and other vegetation. On a downland partridge shoot, where we have killed 150 brace of birds a day to seven guns, there was very little arable land. And while it was true that, in the interests of the shoot, we did hand-feed the birds to

147

some extent, the coveys undoubtedly found good living on the seeds of grass and weeds, showing an inclination to " migrate " towards arable land only a long while after the grass had seeded. This, of course, was the time to encourage them to stay with us by judiciously scattering feed at certain spots.

In days of yore, when farming followed the simple rotation of crops, and intensive partridge preservation as we know it to-day was unheard of, the very great majority of nests hatched round about 20th June. Now, so altered have become conditions generally, that it is by no means uncommon to find broods of partridge chicks in May, in July and even in August (the latter, of course, being the result of second nests where the first have failed, or been destroyed). As an old keeper once put it to me, " if they go on farming like they do, and mess about trying to increase partridges, we shall soon be having them nesting all the year round ! " The cutting of green crops just at the time when birds (and to the sportsman the term " birds," when referring to game, infers partridges) are nesting, accounts for the destruction of countless eggs every year, but my old friend was chiefly concerned with the modern methods of interfering with the natural breeding of partridges.

On big partridge shoots, the so-called Euston system is practised, this, in brief, being the collecting of eggs from nests and the hatching of them under hens or bantams while the mother partridges sit on dummy eggs exchanged for their own. The keeper makes a note of the date on which old birds " go down " (*i.e.* commence to sit) and he is then able to place under them, long before the twenty-fourth and last day of their natural " incubation," eggs that show signs of chipping under a hen. By this complicated method, many broods may be " got away " early and during good weather —big broods of from 15 to 20 chicks. Another advantage is that many eggs are saved from destruction by vermin. I

148

helped to work this system for many years and found it very
satisfactory on downland, but there is no doubt that land can
be overstocked with partridges, and this helps to encourage
disease and other troubles. In its favour, however, it may
be said that, as eggs from so many nests get mixed, there is
less likelihood of in-breeding, while broods " got away "
under suitable weather conditions and eggs saved from
vermin and egg thieves result in many and good coveys
being seen about the ground.

In a book for the young shot a description, however brief,
of this system may seem out of place, but I have a good
reason for mentioning it—a reason that will be doubly clear
if a keeper can be persuaded to allow you to accompany him
on his round of nests and to show you the workings of it.
There is, in fact, no way of becoming so intimately acquainted
with the characteristics of partridges. To start with, nests
have to be found, and this is usually accomplished by walking
down grassy banks and likely fences, seeking out with
practised eye those runs which lead to them. A long wand is
used for carefully parting the herbage during the search,
and often a nest that is overlooked while walking down a
fence is discovered when walking back along the same side.
The nest itself is formed of a thin layer of grass and leaves,
and some of this " litter " is used by the sitting bird to cover
her eggs while she is off feeding. I suppose 12 to 14 olive
eggs may be said to be the average number per nest, but a
nest may contain anything from 10 to 20. After a few eggs
have been laid, one or two are collected and wooden dummies,
shaped and painted to resemble the genuine article, are placed
in the nest. This operation requires a certain amount of
care, for a laying partridge will desert her nest far more
easily than a sitting one. Accordingly, the exchange is done
when the hen is away, or when the birds have been flushed
and have flown some distance.

The time you learn most about the partridge, however, is

when eggs, taken from under the foster-mother as they show signs of chipping, are returned to the sitting partridge. Individual birds react in different ways. I have returned some eggs to nests by gradually inserting my hand along the run and under the old partridge, which remained sitting. The majority of partridges will not allow so intimate an operation, but will run off the nest for a foot or two and squat there, hissing threats. Still others, and happily they are very few, if due care is not taken, will suddenly fly up like a rocket and may desert the nest altogether. But partridges, like pheasants, or almost any wild creature, get used to a person whom they see regularly and who obviously does not intend to harm them. Consequently, while the keeper is able to make this exchange of eggs, quite another story might result if a stranger attempted it.

Partridges are the most devoted of parents, as witness how a mother bird will risk her life to draw danger away from her brood. Flopping about the ground with an apparently broken wing, and uttering loud cries, she attracts the full attention of man, fox, dog or vermin to her " wounded " state, and, not until she has led the intruder some distance from her young does she make a sudden recovery and fly away, remaining hidden for a time before returning to her chicks.

But it is at hatching time that we see the parents at their best. As eggs hatch and still more young work their way out of the shells, the cock bird snuggles down close to the hen and takes over some of the family, brooding them until they are dry and fit to be led away into the safety of the nearest cover. Alas, when heavy storms break suddenly and broods are caught in the long wet grass among which they find it difficult to move about, casualties occur, but when living among the corn, the old birds lead their young down the drills to the better shelter of the hedgerows and casualties are usually avoided. Nor do partridges, like pheasants, expect their young to trail after them through thick and thin. The partridge shows every concern for her brood, frequently stopping to assure herself that all are safe. The pheasant, on the other hand, is a bad mother, and as long as she is aware that some of her brood are in tow, she continues her way through soaking herbage and other difficult cover and so loses a proportion if not the whole of her brood in bad weather. Often, too, I have seen a sitting or a brooding partridge fluffing herself out and hissing in wrath as cattle or sheep wandered too close to her nest, or brood. She is utterly fearless in defence of her young and is as devoted a wife and mother as any bird I know.

The young sportsman, keen to get on terms with the coveys on his ground, should make an exhaustive study of the habits of the partridge under varying climatic conditions. Soon after daybreak the calling partridges will commence to feed, flying or running from those spots where they juk at night. A juking covey sit tail to tail, their heads facing outwards in a protective circle. When the weather is hot, this circle becomes wider, contracting into a mere ball of feathers during a cold night as the partridges snuggle against each other for warmth. Evidence of this is plain in the form in which the droppings of the birds can be seen at the spot where they jukked. In January, if the weather is mild, the coveys begin to pair, as the droppings of pairs about a small area where the family has hitherto slept clearly show. Should a cold spell set in, the paired birds may return to covey formation.

At dawn, then, the partridges are calling and feeding about the fields, but as the sun rises and its heat is felt, they will seek the cool shelter of the grass and reeds in the water, meadows, or rest among the roots. It is useless to plod mile after mile across plough, stubble or other " open " ground. Far more profitable to hunt out the damp and shady spots. And when it is wet, the reverse applies. You will seldom find partridges on a wet morning among the kale, the mangolds, the turnips, the beet and the lush grass of the low meadows. Again, on a morning when a cold wind or rain soughs across the fallows, prepare to find the coveys sheltering in the lee of fences and banks, or in old pits and hollows.

Partridges make their second feed in the afternoon, continuing to fill their crops until the winter's twilight tells them that jukking time is close at hand. Then, after a few calls, they rise on wing and silently make for the meadow or the field where they spend the night. Every sportsman should get to know the whereabouts of the coveys on his ground and where to expect to find them at certain hours of the day. More than this, he should study their lines of flight, so that, when a friend accompanies him on a walk-round, one may attempt to walk up the birds, while the other, taking advantage of the cover of hedge or bush, can wait at a spot along the line the birds are expected to take. Covey-hunting by one or by two shooters has a technique all its own, and though types of ground may differ considerably the main principles remain the same.

Writing of covey-hunting reminds me of a form of shooting that is often termed " covey-hunting," but which is not at all sportsmanlike. During September the young birds of the year have not yet attained full powers of flight, and are apt to get easily tired if driven hither and thither. This especially applies if the weather is hot or muggy. No sportsman worthy the name will shoot partridges little more than half-grown for the larder. Even when the birds are approaching the size of their parents, there is no excuse for driving them from one field to another, and then on to still another field and back again. Time to do this when their powers of flight are fully developed and when their cunning has matured.

What in the first few weeks of the season may be termed shameful later becomes a game at which the partridge often comes off best. Fully matured birds require skill to approach to within range, and further skill is required to get them to fly towards and drop into that patch of roots or that meadow of long grass. But once they have dropped into good cover, the shooter has a better chance of coming upon terms with them.

Generations of sportsmen have been content to agree that a partridge with a prominent chestnut horseshoe on its breast is a cock, and the bird with one far less clearly defined is a hen. Such, I agree, may far more often than not be the case, yet I have seen cock birds with a very poor horseshoe crest and hens that had surprisingly clear ones. Study and make note of the plumage of cock and hen side by side and many differences will be discovered, particularly as spring approaches. The hen has more grey in the head and face, and the red " warts and wattles " of a cock thinking of pairing are not a feature of her make-up.

To tell the difference between old and young partridges is not difficult. During autumn the young birds have a yellowish tinge to their legs and beaks, which later becomes greenish, but is still fairly simple to identify from the slaty grey of the old bird's legs and beak. The best test, however, is to examine the two outer primary feathers of the wing. In young birds, these are pointed, and also shorter before maturity. In the old, they are full-length and rounded at the tops.

The young of partridges, like the young of grouse, are called cheepers. Two dead partridges are known as a brace ; three as a leash. A covey is a family of partridges from the time the brood is able to fly to the time it pairs up for nesting. Coveys that join up, as they sometimes do in hard weather, become a pack.

The Red-legged Partridge.—While it has been said that an odd migrant of this species has occasionally been dis-covered along our east coast, the " Frenchman," as the red-legged partridge is often called, was introduced into this country for sport just before the end of the eighteenth century. Later, it became unpopular, for gossip had it that it harried, fought and often killed our native grey partridge. Consequently, sportsmen and keepers took to destroying its eggs whenever they found them, and the poor bird, probably to its great surprise and regret, became classed as vermin. Happily for it, and for those who now like to see it about the shoot, the crimes laid at its door have since been disproved. Also, since driving has taken the place of walking-up partridges, its trait of running ahead of guns through, say, a field of roots and disturbing or putting up other coveys need no longer be held against it.

Coveys of red-legged partridges are seldom seen on shooting days, the birds rising singly and coming forward swiftly and in a dead straight line, with wings whirring—excellent practice for young shooters.

The " Frenchman's " habit of running often lands it in trouble, for tearing over wet ground in front of beaters, its feet become clogged, or balled, and it is then neither able to rise, nor to make much headway over the ground. Beaters and dogs are able to catch it under these circumstances—unless it darts down a rabbit burrow, a habit that is common with it when hard pressed.

The eggs of the " French " partridge are yellowish with fine red spots and blotches, and from 9 to 18 are laid—sometimes in the top of a haystack. In fact, cases have been recorded of labourers bringing in a clutch of " hawk's " eggs from a rick, only to be told that hawks do not nest in ricks and that the eggs are those of a red-legged.

Another queer trait of the bird is that it will lay an egg or two and then apparently desert the nest, but some days later another egg will make its appearance.

I have one or two friends who for some strange reason (probably advice handed down from their sporting fathers, dislike the red-legged and allow me to remove the eggs of any found on their land. This I do with pleasure, and have taken many coops of this bird to covert with pheasants and they have provided good sport in due season. But you never can be quite sure whether they will "stay put," for, unless they like the type of land, they will soon disappear—migrating quietly, in their own time, to give someone else the benefit of their presence.

CHAPTER SEVENTEEN

Snipe

*Species and Characteristics—Types of Snipe Ground
—Habits of the Common Snipe—A Myth Exploded—
The Art in Snipe Shooting—Methods of Walking-up
—The Right Dog.*

IN the British Isles, we get three definite species of snipe—
the common, full, or whole snipe ; the great, double,
woodcock, or solitary snipe ; the jack, or half snipe.

The common snipe, as its name implies, is the bird we
are most accustomed to see on our moors, marshes and water-
meadows. From autumn until spring our resident stock is
greatly increased by winter visitors, and local migrations take
place even during mild winters. In hard weather, when the
bogs and marshes become frozen, these soft-billed mud-
feeders move southward and westward, filling the Irish bogs
with refugees and providing excellent shooting for sportsmen
in the south and west of England and in Wales. It is then
that, hard put to it to find soft feeding-grounds, odd snipe
or small whisps will be discovered beside ditches and springs
that remain unfrozen, round the muddied broken ice of
gateways through which cattle have passed and, indeed, in
close proximity to human dwellings or farmyards where the
sight of mud or running water attracts their searching eyes.
I have even put up snipe under my own scullery window,
where the waste-water from the sink had overflowed on to
the surrounding frozen ground. I do not doubt that they

were disappointed in what they found, or did not find, there, but it shows how eagerly the birds search all damp spots under the stress of climatic conditions.

The great snipe, breeding in Northern Europe and north-west Asia and wintering from the Mediterranean to the Cape, is better expressed as a passing migrant to the British Isles, rather than a winter visitor. In England it is most frequently seen in early autumn. In Scotland and Ireland it is rare. I think the name " woodcock snipe " describes this bird better than its others, for not only does it resort to drier places than our other snipe, such as bracken and woodlands, but its manner of flight is not unlike the woodcock's, being heavier and slower than that of the common species and entirely free from the zigzag tactics so successfully adopted by its cousins of the marshes and sloblands. Also, its bill is comparatively short. I have never had the opportunity of studying this bird in its breeding-haunts, but it is said that it does not " drum " like the common snipe while displaying, but is capable of uttering several notes. When flushed, it rises silently from the ground. Actually, there are few sportsmen of my acquaintance who have come across this bird, or, if they have, they failed to recognise it in flight.

The diminutive jack snipe is a regular and common visitor to our shores from early autumn until spring. Reports of nests of this species being found in the British Isles have, I believe, no foundation in fact. It is said by some writers that the jack snipe, on being flushed, rises without sound and does not zigzag in the manner of the common snipe. These statements are not altogether true, however, for I have many times heard a jack snipe utter a weak plaintive call on rising, although others have remained silent. As to its manner of flight, its zigzags are by no means as exaggerated as those of its larger cousin and may perhaps be best described as deliberate dodges. The most marked feature of the jack snipe, apart from its size and flight (and its size by comparison with that of the full snipe is not always easy to ascertain when it rises), is its common habit of lying low until almost trodden upon, when it springs up and flies off in no great hurry, dropping down again after a short flight.

Thus, I well remember in my youthful days imagining a shot at a jack snipe had taken effect because the bird settled within a hundred yards or so. When I made for and reached the spot, however, up sprang the snipe again, to be missed with the single-barrelled ·410 I carried, and this performance continued until perhaps three or four shots had been fired and the bird, feeling justifiably annoyed at being thus harassed, finally departed out of sight, or dropped down on the far side of a brook and so defeated its pursuer.

Some sportsmen prefer to leave the jack snipe alone, when they recognise it, stating it to be an easy target and hardly large enough to be worthy of an honoured place on the dining-room table. I admit that this bird is not difficult to hit, although, according to some people, it often seems to find a gap in the pattern of shots ! Still, as a tasty morsel on the menu it is not to be despised, and I cannot find myself condemning the sportsman who records it in his shooting diary at the finish of the day.

There can be little advantage, I think, in describing in detail the plumage of the three species of snipe. These will be found in any book on birds. There is one feature, however, of the three snipe that is interesting and worth mentioning— the tail. The common snipe has, as a rule, fourteen tail-feathers, their basal portion black and the tips red, except for the outer pair which have white ends. All the feathers are marked with a subterminal black band. The great snipe has sixteen tail-feathers, the greater part of the outer ones being white towards the tip. The jack snipe has twelve tail-feathers only, these being more pointed than those of the other species, particularly the pair in the centre. They are dark brown with reddish margins. Incidentally, the bill of the little jack snipe is quite an inch and a half shorter than that of the common snipe. The foregoing details of tail plumage may be of little use when watching the flying bird, but they certainly form a means of identification when, and if for some reason, the species of dead bird is in doubt.

Undoubtedly the best and most profitable snipe grounds in the British Isles are the Irish bogs, for here, in comparative peace, the birds can live, probing and feeding in the soft oozy ground with their long sensitive bills. There are, however, many marshes in England, Scotland and Wales, where first-rate snipe shooting may be enjoyed, even water-meadows beside rivers and brooks producing good bags in suitable seasons, as I shall show later.

Worms are the snipe's staple diet, though insects and certain minor inhabitants of the mud are also taken. In daytime, the birds lay up among the reed-tussocks of marsh-land and similar cover, flighting at dusk to their favoured feeding-grounds—soft mud beside rivers, lakes, ponds and ditches ; in fact, any boggy situation into which their bills can probe with ease. Where snipe feed by night, countless splashes of white on the ground mark their activities, and there will be seen, too, those small holes in the ground, or in the leavings of cattle, which the snipe have " bored " overnight, and such evidence should not be overlooked by the observant sportsman.

In some respects, the habits of snipe are not unlike those of duck. They are both night-feeders, laying up quietly by day. As dusk approaches, a snipe will rise from one of a thousand small tufts of reeds pushing their head through a flooded portion of the marsh, and with a note, almost of invitation, will fly off towards the feeding-grounds. Fully awake now, other snipe follow, singly, by twos and threes, or in larger whisps, until the daytime habitat is empty of bird life, except for sleepy pippits and perhaps a few lark, and those distant banks by river, pond and ditch awake to the arrival of snipe " talking " harshly among themselves as they drop down to feed.

During hard weather, when hunger has driven the snipe to make long journeys southwards and westwards, I have watched birds fall out of the sky, as it were, and land close to the edge of an open spring. For perhaps a minute they remain almost motionless, as if straining every sense to take in the situation and discover if danger is present. Suddenly, the tension relaxes and first one and then another runs with quick steps to the water's edge and, without more ado, commences probing with its bill, " feeling " for the food which puts new life and vigour into a tired and hungry body.

While the wide boglands, the fens and the marshes (even the sewage farms) may be described as typical haunts of snipe, both on account of the available food supply and the natural short cover in close proximity, the coarse grass and reed-tussocks of some water-meadows provide the most excellent snipe-shooting except in time of drought, when the ground becomes too hard for feeding purposes. I say " some " water-meadows advisedly, for I know of chains of riverside meadows where snipe are seldom seen, ever after a flood, while other meadows hold the snipe year after year and in such quantities that any snipe shooter should be well satisfied to have the shooting over such a pasture. As an instance of this, just over ten years ago, in a winter of exceptionally hard weather, I shot to my own gun on less than 48 acres of water-meadow, no less than 389 snipe. Fifty to 150 snipe a year was not an unusual figure for this favoured bit of ground, but in that particular season I took advantage of the southward and later the return migration to visit my meadows three or four times a day from the time the hard weather lasted to the time when it seemed a majority of the birds driven south had returned.

Strangely enough, you can often take a chain of water-meadows and find that while any amount of snipe may be

Young shots walking up grouse in Skye

A young shot with a fine pheasant

found at suitable times in this one and that one, there are
others which it is a waste of time to walk up (at least, for snipe)
as a snipe will rarely be found there. It might be supposed
that the reason lay in the matter of suitable cover, or disturbance by grazing beasts. Not so, however, for I know

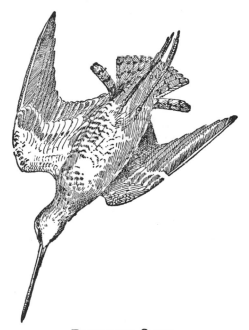

DRUMMING SNIPE

meadows that resemble each other exactly, so far as cover,
etc., are concerned, but the snipe flock to some and leave
others severely alone. There is some mystery here for which
I will not suggest a satisfactory solution.

The common snipe nests in the water-meadows as well
as on more suitable ground. In spring, I have discovered
three or four nests in quite a small meadow, moreover,

M

bordered with lush green grass, its centre a pattern of reed-tussocks. Here, where kingcup, buttercup, moon-daisy, cuckoo-flower and orchis bloom and the nesting plover wail and tumble overhead, the snipe makes its grass-lined cup of a nest well in the shelter of the reeds and lays its four pyriform eggs, their small ends turned towards the centre of the nest, as also do those of the plover.

Throughout the spring and summer days, the curious drumming of courting and nesting snipe may be heard overhead, difficult to tell from the bleat of a kid, but caused through that downward rush of the circling, mounting bird, with wings half open and tail-feathers wide spread. Both in the air and on the ground during the season of display and courtship the snipe utters a call that is best described as " chipper-chipper, chipper-chipper, chipper-chipper." When uttering these notes from the prominence of a post or rail, it will be noticed that the head of the bird moves up and down in rhythm, or it bobs and bows in a manner more often associated with the redshank. So much for a brief sketch of our snipe, their more common habits and the type of ground on which they are found, without which simple knowledge, however, the sport of snipe-shooting would be less pleasant and less successful !

It is my firm opinion (and I feel I should add with due modesty that I have done my fair share of snipe-shooting) that the common and oft-repeated saying that snipe are the most difficult birds to hit, and that only experts at the game can be assured of reasonable success, is a myth that demands immediate exploding. Many young snipe shots have been " put off " their shooting by the very natural nervousness or anxiety they feel, especially when an onlooker is present, when remembering these stories of the evasive snipe and the necessity to shoot the bird the moment it springs from cover. There is also that contrary advice which states that you should wait until the bird has stopped zigzagging before you press

SNIPE

the trigger. Between these bits of practical(?) advice comes
that of the humourist who tells you that you should never
shoot when the snipe zigs, or when it zags, but should press
the trigger when the bird is in a central position between the
zig and the zag !

My advice to young snipe shooters is to forget all such
instructions, whether delivered seriously or in humour and
to think the matter out for themselves in conjunction with
their own experiences. It is perfectly true that the snipe is
often an evasive bird, particularly when it is wide awake and
wild, rising far ahead of the advancing shooter and zigzagging
like mad, before it climbs heavenwards to swing unsteadily,
a black mote against the blue of the sky. It is equally true
to say that the shooter who has not got a firm control of his
nerves, or who is apt to fire before he has properly steadied
himself both physically and mentally, will find himself missing
his snipe again and again. And each time he misses, the more
exasperated he will become, to the detriment of " aim."
The snipe is a small target and one that often plays tricks
designed to put the shooter off his guard. It seldom gives
you time to collect your thoughts, although the sportsman in
the process of walking-up snipe should have his thoughts
already concentrated on the job in hand.

The secret of successful snipe-shooting is this. Having
thrust from mind all friendly advice on the subject, make up
your mind not to get flurried at any cost when snipe rise. If
you think you are sufficiently experienced in snap-shooting,
having done a lot of this at rabbits in thick cover, or at vermin
birds among the trees of the covert, then by all means try
taking your snipe just as quickly as you can when they spring
from the ground. If you find you can kill a fair percentage
in this way, well and good, for when birds are rising wild
at extreme ranges, it is to be admitted that the man who
can snap them then will have a great advantage over the
slower, more deliberate shot who will have to let those far-

rising birds go, they being out of range before he can get on to them. It is to be admitted, too, that a majority of the most successful snipe-shooters do " snap " their birds as soon as they rise. On the other hand, I know a number of first-class snipe shots who never hurry to shoot when a bird springs suddenly from the cover ahead. Deliberately the gun goes up and at what appears to be the most convenient moment to the shooter, the trigger is pressed and down comes the bird. As I have said, this type of shot may not be so successful on a morning when the snipe are wild and rising far ahead, but his calm deliberation very often scores him a hit when the " snap " shooter might be just a little too hasty and the snipe escape his charge of shot.

I, myself, confess to being a slow shot on snipe, so that perhaps a hint or two from my point of view may be useful. When snipe feed by moonlight, they quickly satisfy their hunger and are able to retire to rest long before the sun rises. Having rested well, they will be alive and inclined to wildness during the morning when you are walking the marsh in their pursuit, particularly if they are in whisps. When, however, the night is pitch dark and perhaps rough, the birds are forced to feed at dawn and may even be found satisfying their hunger an hour or so later. On such mornings, they will be tired and will be found to be anything but " quick on the uptake." They may sit until one is almost on top of them and even then rise with a sluggishness that makes them far easier targets than when they are well fed and well rested. Now, there are times when a snipe zigzags like a flash of lightning, but there are also times when its zigzag is more like the lazy dodging flight of the little jack snipe. Probably the foregoing conditions of feeding and resting have a bearing on this, a well-fed and well-rested snipe getting off the mark quickly and zigzagging with the vitality of alert senses, while a tired bird does not put so much energy into its powers of flight. Snipe that have flown far on migration may show an equal reluctance to rise and to zigzag, for they are tired and possibly hungry, or they may have spent the night in flight and the early morning in feeding. A snipe that is sluggish is not a difficult target, either for the " snap " shooter or the more deliberate shot ; that is, if he does not allow himself to be flustered just because the bird *is* a snipe and the general opinion is that snipe are the most difficult birds to shoot.

The " snap " shooter usually kills his snipe before it gets into its most erratic form of flight, but here it is that the slower shot (slower by nature or slower by deliberate design) has the opportunity to experiment, as it were, with his shooting and, if he finds he has been missing his birds, to correct his faults. In those few seconds it takes a snipe to rise from the ground and fly its zigzag course over forty or fifty yards, there should be ample time for the shooter to do quite a lot of thinking, if only he will learn to master any natural excitement and train himself to shoot coolly and deliberately. Having missed several snipe, he must try and ascertain in his own mind what he is doing wrong and, when he imagines he may be able to supply the answer, he should experiment along these lines in those few available seconds that the next bird offers him. If he finds himself still missing, a further debate should be held with himself and further deliberate (cold-blooded, if you like) experiments be tried. If no one is present, it does not matter if birds are missed in a good cause ! By these means it will soon be found which method, the " snap " or " wait," better suits the shooter.

One thing is certain, and that is that no hard-and-fast rules can be laid down for the successful killing of snipe. Each sportsman must experiment for himself, choose his own style and his own time for pressing the trigger, and when he finds he can kill snipe in a certain way, then he should stick to that way, whatever well-meaning advice may be offered him relating to style, etc.

In walking-up snipe, it is a mistake to hurry. If the ground is comparatively dry, walk slowly forward, and even slacken the pace when approaching spots where snipe are known to lay. Snipe have favourite spots of this kind where they lay up to rest, and it is here that one will find them day after day, although it serves a useful purpose not to " over shoot " such places. Like all other birds, snipe dislike being harassed, and may altogether desert a place that is disturbed and shot too frequently.

It is a matter for controversy and local conditions whether snipe should be walked up- or down-wind, or even across-wind. The birds, when flushed, naturally rise into the wind. This means that if you are walking against the wind, the snipe will fly away from you, its speed lessened by the wind, and you also have the advantage that the wind has deadened any sound of your approach, so that you have been able to get well within range of your birds. Also, the report of your gun will be blown back and may have a less disturbing effect on birds lying ahead. On the other hand, if you walk the marsh down-wind, while the birds may hear your approach, and the sound of shooting may disturb the place, the snipe that do rise within range will not fly many yards before they commence to turn back into the wind, thus offering the easiest type of target, the crossing shot. By walking across-wind, one gets a mixture of both kinds of shots, with other angles thrown in. If variety is the spice of sport, then commend me to this method, although I prefer as a general rule being influenced by existing circumstances. By this, I mean that if snipe are wild, it is useless walking them down-wind, for they will probably, hearing your approach, rise out of shot and the report of your gun will set every snipe in the marsh on the alert, if not in the air. If, however, the birds are sleepy and sluggish, the down-wind method of approach is to be commended. Wild snipe are definitely best walked up-wind, for not only can you approach unheard, but a majority of birds will be within game-shooting distance when you press the trigger.

In a later chapter I have explained how a dog is not only useful, but a necessity on most marshes where game and duck are shot and may be lost as " runners," or by falling in, or over water. When, however, one is stalking snipe on a quiet day and wading ankle-deep in flood-water, one's own slow approach is somewhat cancelled by the pad-padding, splash-splashing of the dog. It is very necessary, therefore, that the dog used for snipe-shooting should be under strict control, to prevent it running into shot with a great splashing that will disturb birds over a wide area, or be left to sit, tied or untied, while its master moves forward to the more likely spots.

Where snipe are plentiful and conditions allow, the birds may be driven over a hedge, or belt of trees, and it is then surprising how badly their height and speed of flight can be misjudged. It is probable that the birds are at first higher than they look and moving faster than their short wing-beats make you believe. But whether moving faster or slower than they appear, their height and speed will certainly increase as shooting commences. Driven snipe, to be successfully bagged, require more practice and experiment than might at first be thought, probably because one seldom gets the opportunity of enjoying this form of shooting, and partly because the size of the birds, compared to that of game, wildfowl and pigeon, make them deceptive targets.

CHAPTER EIGHTEEN

The Woodcock

*Habits and Characteristics of the Woodcock—Some
Mysteries concerning it—The Woodcock in Sport—
When the 'Cock are " in "—Woodcock Shooting.*

THE shooting of my first woodcock must be registered
against me as an unintentional " crime." It was a late
winter's twilight and I had, I remember, arranged to meet
the keeper at his hut in the big wood. I had arrived at the
hut half an hour before the appointed time and wandered up
the ride as far as the cattle hurdle that served as a gate.
There I stood, watching the rabbits feeding and playing in
the meadow at the edge of the wood, at the same time being
alert for a shot at a pigeon, a jay or a hawk. I had not been
there long when a peculiar sound attracted my attention.
It seemed to issue from the ash-poles on my right, but defied
interpretation. It was almost immediately repeated, and this
time it appeared to come from above the poles, and was much
nearer. Next minute, a shadowy form, silent of wing at the
distance of about twenty yards, issued from the shadow of
the wood and showed against the skyline over the meadow.
Either a little owl or a hawk I decided, and immediately
brought off a quick and accurate shot.

As I fumbled to undo the fastening of the hurdle, two
similar birds flitted into sight and made off silently against
the dark background of the meadow. I admit I was at a
loss to solve the mystery of their identity, for I quickly
realised that neither three little owls nor three hawks would

be seen under these circumstances, although the actions of
the birds in flight might have belonged to either species.
On picking up the dead bird, however, I was surprised and
somewhat shocked to discover it was a woodcock. Surprised,
as I had little experience of woodcock in those days and
somehow could not imagine seeing three together. Shocked,
because the average number of woodcock seen in the wood

WOODCOCK

was two per season, and I had strict orders from the keeper
not to kill woodcock, however great the temptation. When
the keeper eventually arrived and I made my explanation, he
was more amused than annoyed and explained that the birds
" were arodin'," a subject which I will explain a little later on.
    This experience aroused a natural curiosity in me, and,
on returning home, I searched every available book on sport
in order to get a better knowledge of a bird that had seldom

come my way, and of which I knew little beyond the fact that the killing of one, or perhaps two, in the course of a day's covert shooting in our part of the county caused no little excitement, and that the appearance of woodcock at a shoot, even where they were far from rare, was spoken of by older guns as an event that stirred the pulses even of experienced sportsmen.

Since that far away day, I have shot woodcock in many counties, have discussed their ways with various eminent sportsmen and naturalists and though I may say that I know perhaps a little more about them than the average man who carries a gun, I admit that we have yet a lot to learn concerning a very interesting and evasive bird, as I shall show.

From September onwards, almost to the end of the year, big flights of woodcock arrive from over the North Sea, to add to the many that are resident in the British Isles, returning to their breeding-grounds during March and April. By that time, the birds that are resident in this country are not only nesting, but are sitting on their four eggs in a scraped-out depression in the ground, both bird and eggs well camouflaged by the leaves and twigs that carpet the woods and coverts, or by the dead bracken against which the plumage of a sitting woodcock is difficult to locate. A sharp eye, however, may sometimes discern the big eye of the woodcock as she covers her eggs, this feature of the bird being set well back in the head.

I have been told by more than one keeper well acquainted with the woodcock at nesting time that the bird turns on her eggs as the sun crosses the heavens, and that otherwise the sunlight striking the big eyes would so reflect on them that vermin would immediately spot the sitting bird. By turning on her nest, and so keeping her back towards the sun, she avoids drawing attention to herself to her possible undoing. Whether or not this is true of individual birds that dislike the sun shining in their eyes, I cannot say, but I have taken the trouble to observe several sitting woodcock at different periods of the morning and am bound to record although the day was bright the birds remained in the same position on their eggs.

The ringing of woodcock (that is light rings being placed on the legs of nestling birds) has proved that, while some birds seem to stay for years about the same locality where they were hatched, others move about the country and a great number are found in Ireland.

In many respects, the woodcock's habits resemble those of the snipe, although the bird itself is considerably larger than the " long-bill." While choosing drier spots wherein to lie up by day, such as the heather of moorland, bracken covered hills, woods and coverts (where it seems to enjoy the shelter of such cover as that provided by rhododendron and holly bushes, being well sheltered and protected from dripping boughs in time of rain) it flights at dusk to places where the feeding is soft, probing, as does the snipe, in the mud and ooze for worms. At daybreak, it returns to the dry shelter it left at dusk, and it is my experience that, like the snipe, its vitality and behaviour when flushed by day depends upon the conditions of night feeding. If birds have suffered a rough or pitch dark night and have been forced to feed at dawn, they will retire to their daytime shelter tired out, to sit comparatively tight and rise sluggishly when flushed, but show a readiness to rise on approaching disturbance and a quicker dodging flight when they have fed well and returned early to rest.

Often after the long migratory flight across the North Sea, woodcock arrive on these shores tired out and in a state of semi-starvation. The term " a fall " of woodcock usually denotes when these birds have arrived in known winter haunts, but I can imagine the term having been coined (and I stand to be corrected) when woodcock have literally fallen on to our east coast. If the weather has been hard in their northern haunts, the birds are in poor condition even before the long journey commences. By the time they reach these shores, they are then quite unworthy of powder and shot. They creep into the nearest cover available and may be picked up by dogs, or knocked over with sticks. At other times, when they have fared better, the journey over land and sea may tire them, but in a few hours they have recovered and continued their flight, scattering over the British Isles, and taking up quarters in those woods and coverts where we discover them and remark, with some show of excitement, that " the 'cock are in."

Under normal conditions, it is to be supposed that most big movements of birds are undertaken under cover of darkness and one wonders at what speed a bird like the woodcock, which under normal conditions is a dawdler rather than a fast flier, travels over the sea. The late Mr. T. A. Coward, that great ornithologist, tells us that the speed is great, and instances an occasion when a woodcock on migration crashed through the lanthorn at the Flamborough Light. Incidentally, it may here be remarked that since bird perches were erected and maintained on lighthouses, millions of feathered migrants of every species have been saved. Attracted by the bright light, the migrants would fly into and flutter round the " lanthorn," like moths round a lamp, finally to fall tired out into the sea below and perish miserably. The erection of perches and wire-netting prevent this wholesale destruction and the birds that fall into the netting are, in due course, able to continue their flight.

As I have pointed out, the woodcock is an early nester, but before that event, we witness a most interesting display of courtship known as " roding." Unhappily, as I discovered on enquiry, it was a woodcock on one of these love flights that I had shot that early morning at the edge of the wood. During these morning and evening flights, the birds are said to travel over the same course day after day and that the course is usually triangular. Be that as it may, I do know that the same course is followed and at approximately the same time, when the birds are " roding," and that several different sounds are uttered by them in a croaking voice, while at regular intervals there comes what can only be described as a screech.

One seldom hears the term " 'cock-roads " used nowadays, but these refer to the favourite courses taken by " roding " woodcock. In the bad old days, nets, known as " 'cock-nets," were hung between trees in certain rides down which the 'cock flew, and this unsporting method of catching a most sporting bird must have helped to denude many woods and coverts of woodcock. I have myself used these nets, but for a more worthy purpose. Like the woodcock, the sparrow-hawk has certain rides down which it loves to rush at dusk, though in its case there is no love in the heart. Once it can be ascertained by observation which are the hawk's favourite narrow ride, a thin net placed across it will surely intercept that daring raider and it will be found entangled in the meshes. On the Continent, in countries where the etiquette of sport is less strict than it is here, and the size of the bag is given first consideration, the woodcock is shot during its courting flights, a fact that is to be deplored.

There are many authorities who declare that the wood-cock is given the instinct and ability to carry its young to and from the feeding-grounds between its thighs. A number claim to have witnessed this feat. On the other hand, there are several keepers of my acquaintance, looking after estates on which many woodcock nest, who declare that, despite years of experience of nesting woodcock, they have yet to see the bird perform such a feat. They will admit to the bird flying with tail fanned but depressed and bill down-pointed, which mode of flight, they declare, may have given rise to the belief that young were being transported. But why, they ask, should the woodcock and not the snipe and other waders be given this particular facility? Then come stories from the opposing camp of thought of woodcock and their young making an appearance in walled-in gardens, where escape, except by air, is impossible, yet the young are taken outside to feed and brought safely back. For myself, I am content to await the day, if it arrives, when this feat of the woodcock is photographed by some patient man, whose name, no doubt, will never be forgotten by ornithologists or bird photographers. When experts and specialists fall out, their evidence differing, though we must not doubt their words, it is difficult, unless one's own eyes back one up, to form an opinion. Therefore, although I have my own theories concerning the question of the woodcock carrying its young, I prefer to remain silent on the point.

It is said by some naturalists that the woodcock, in order to rise, places its beak against the ground and somersaults into the air. Others deny this. Possibly the true explanation lies in the fact that the bird sits on the ground, its bill held downwards and compressed against its breast. When suddenly disturbed, the appearance of the bill in this position and the " ripping " sound of its wings as it springs from the earth may give a somewhat false impression, and I have myself wondered at times if I was not witnessing a new form of " take-off."

Another curious thing about the bird, and one about which no definite decision appears to have been made, is the position of the ears, which are below and forward of the eyes. Whether these assist its hearing it is difficult to say, but since its feeding habits and food are similar to those of the snipe, there may be some other explanation for this unusual feature.

Still another interesting thing about the woodcock is that the sex of an adult bird cannot be told, except by dissection. Some experts claim to tell the difference in sex between very young birds, but it is often uncertain that they are correct in their assumptions.

THE WOODCOCK

That the woodcock is a sporting bird goes without saying. Its presence in the game cart after a covert shoot delights every one. Not only is it a bird of beauty, the colour and markings of its plumage being in perfect harmony with the russets and shades of its natural surroundings, but the minor mysteries that surround its life, the strange effect its appearance has on the nerves of even experienced sportsmen, and last, but not least, its very edible qualities, combine to place it in a category all its own. Even the woodcock's pin-feathers, small sharp feathers found near the angle of the wings at the base of the first primary feathers, are worn with pride in the hat-bands of sportsmen, though some, I fear, are content to wear the " pin-feathers " of hen pheasants that at first glance much resemble those of the woodcock. The pin-feather of the woodcock, however, is sharper and the markings differ, so that the quick eye need not be taken in by such an exhibition of false pride.

Is the woodcock a really difficult bird to shoot and, if so, why ? This question has repeatedly been put to me by youthful sportsmen. Of necessity, the reply must be somewhat involved. First, let us regard the flight of the bird. When " roding " in the spring, in courtship flight, the 'cock goes through all manner of aerobatics—twisting, darting, rolling and sometimes flapping along like an owl blinded by the daylight. This demonstration of its ability to perform evasive tricks in the air should prepare us for evasive flight in due season when a woodcock rises from the undergrowth of the wood and goes twisting and darting away between the tree-trunks. When that occurs, only the cool shot will floor his bird. It is ten to one that the presence of a woodcock came as a surprise, unless, of course, the shooter had previously seen one there and was deliberately looking for it, or the fact that there were woodcock to be found in that particular beat of the wood kept him on the sharp look-out. The sudden and unexpected appearance of the bird, however, with the attendant excitement and the fact that the target is making rapidly off in dodging flight may well shake the nerves, when calm and calculated shooting " aim " will go by the board. The cool shot may be surprised, but will immediately collect and marshal his senses and will either " snap " his bird as it passes between the trunks of two trees, or will, being a deliberate shot, subconsciously note a good opening ahead of the departing 'cock and will press the trigger only when he is certain that his charge of shot will catch the bird at the right moment and before it puts yet another tree-trunk between itself and danger.

Such shooting may be compared with that of shooting rabbits as they make off through a plantation of ash-poles. As the rabbit dashes between the stumps, the cool brain of the shooter judges (though sometimes misjudges, I fear !) just that split second when to press the trigger as the rabbit is about to pass between two stumps. In short, the senses, in telegraphic communication with the brain, have to perform a lightning calculation—a calculation which involves judging the speed of the departing target, whether it is about to dodge to the right or left, and noting what open spots lie ahead of it whichever way it turns and of allowing the necessary allowance or " lead " so that the charge of shots arrives at the most likely place at the same time as the target. If the first barrel misses, those calculations, with the added consideration of longer-range shooting, have to be re-made in a flash, and let us hope that the second barrel takes effect ! If a double miss is registered, the senses must not be allowed to wander and idly study the now distant woodcock or rabbit, but must be placed on the alert for the possibility of a second bird or rabbit tempting providence. To deliberate on or to mourn over a lost opportunity of this kind has all too often led to a second chance being lost, when there will be a very good reason both to deliberate and mourn !

In the open, the woodcock is less given to dodging flight,

176

and will often flap away with that owl-like flight that, never-theless, by its very apparent simplicity, proves deceptive. Many the time I have seen a woodcock missed that merely seemed to be flapping ahead of the gun. Excitement, and possibly over-confidence at so simple a shot, proved salvation for the bird, though a beater nearby is probably heard to exclaim that he could have knocked it down with a stick !

Some of the best woodcock days I have enjoyed, though I usually prefer to wander round with a gun and dog on my own, searching likely spots for these birds, have been spent in bolder-strewn, bracken-clad woods on dry frosty winter days when the " 'cock are in " and a few " back-end " pheasants are to be shot. The woods which particularly dwell in mind border a famous moor and are composed chiefly of oak-scrub, birch and just that right type of under-growth, including patches of evergreen specially planted at spots favoured by woodcock, which offer the birds good shelter and what may be described as " easy rising vantage." By this latter expression I infer that woodcock like to remain dry and sheltered, but to be in a position to rise quickly and without that undue obstruction which tangled underwood may cause them.

Through the valleys of these woods run springs and streams which, in wet weather, become swollen as they receive the cascades of water falling from the higher rock-strewn places. Bracken, in patches, runs from the stone walls of the woods higher boundary down to the deepest valleys, and the rides are wide and well kept, offering pleasant shooting as a pheasant flashes over, or a 'cock comes dodging between the low, stunted oaks. Standing silently in an open, steeply inclined ride, the gun listens to beaters in the distance and presently the cry of " 'cock forrard " reaches the ears. There is time now to steady the nerves before the bat-like bird is seen approaching through a mist of birch-twigs. Here is a good opportunity to take your woodcock in front and without committing the folly of dangerous shooting. Perhaps, though, stouter branches of other trees deny you such a shot and in no time the 'cock is on top of you and behind you and you swing round to kill him in the rear, congratulating yourself that you manœuvred your stand so that a clear space was in the rear for taking shots that have passed over.

In the chestnut woods of the south I have also enjoyed excellent woodcock shooting, though the flat woods, beautiful enough in their own way, did not make the same appeal to the senses as those of the north and, whatever may be said to the contrary, environment counts for a very great deal to the appreciative mind which every true sportsman should possess.

Although I have shot woodcock in many places, the only right and left it has been my good fortune to bring off was at a roadside hedge in Berkshire where one would not, in the ordinary way, expect to find a woodcock. It so happened, however, that the weather had been hard in the north, and at a spot in this hedge was an open spring. As the spaniel worked the fence for a rabbit, a woodcock rose from the spring and set off towards a wood on the far side of the meadow. Before I shot, a second bird sprang from the same spot, and I caught it with the second barrel as it topped the hedge. This incident illustrates the possibilities that hard weather so often brings in its wake.

It is said that when the cry of " 'cock forrard " is heard during a shooting day, the safest thing to do is to lie flat, or get behind a big tree-trunk ! The reason for this " timely " advice is, of course, that the unexpected presence of a woodcock causes much excitement, especially among less experienced guns, and that rash shooting may follow when the bird comes into view. Happily, the circulation of such advice seems to have had a good effect on most sportsmen, for it is my experience that one is far more likely to get " peppered " at a rabbit shoot in covert than when a woodcock is announced !

One final point. The first action of a sportsman who downs a woodcock may be to search for the pin-feathers (sometimes known as the " points ") of the bird, but his next action should be to break the legs just above the " knee-joint " and draw the sinews. The thigh of the woodcock is supposed to be a great delicacy, and for that reason this operation is apparently necessary. I have come across sportsmen with little or no experience of the woodcock who were surprised to discover this point of shooting-field " etiquette," but only once have I known a keeper ignorant of the procedure. As we examined the day's bag of pheasants dangling from the poles stretched across the game-cart he touched the one woodcock with his stick and, turning to me, remarked, " Somebody's given this bird a packet ; they've blown both legs off ! " Needless to say, his keepering activities had been confined to open land and, for some strange reason, he had never seen a woodcock shot in his fifty years of life. He must, I think, be the only keeper living who did not know how to behave towards a dead woodcock on a shooting day.

CHAPTER NINETEEN

The Hare

*The Hare in Sport — Hare Shooting — Range and
" Lead "—The Three Species—" Mad March Hares "
—Some Amusing Side-lights—Habits and Character-
istics—When Hares are Scarce—A Warning.*

NEARLY every beast and bird that is of particular
interest to the sportsman deserves a chapter of its
own, and perhaps, one day, a big work of this kind will attract
the energy of a sporting scribe. Within the limitations of
this book, I have endeavoured to outline the more interesting
and instructive facts concerning the most important animals
and birds that the sportsman pursues, but, of necessity, the
description of others with their individual habits and characteristics, such as those of the many species of wildfowl, has
been brief indeed. Some may say that the hare deserves a
larger chapter than does the woodcock, and yet I have given
that sporting bird more prominence than the hare. My
reason for so doing is that the young sportsman will have
far more opportunity for himself to study the ways of hares,
while the woodcock, except to the fortunate few who live in
first-rate woodcock country, will have little chance to witness
the various peculiarities of this bird.

The great majority of sportsmen are by no means keen
on hare-shooting, especially when the hares are driven to
them. But hares, like rabbits, can become too numerous and
are capable of doing serious damage to farm crops, market
gardens and young plantations. Even the gardener has been

180

known to say hard things concerning a hare that has entered his garden overnight and enjoyed a feast of carnations, pinks, nasturtiums, or parsley. Also, hares, when allowed to become numerous, contract various unpleasant diseases, so that in their own interests, it is necessary to reduce a stock that is becoming too large.

In some parts of the country hares are scarce; in others they are too plentiful. In one large field, facing a house in which I lived at the foot of the Berkshire downs, I one day counted seventy hares during the mating season. Two days of hare driving over the downs, with some twenty guns out, used to yield us close on a thousand hares. When this number is added to those shot throughout the season during partridge driving, and to the great number we would find dead after they had feasted on young frosted clover, it will be readily seen how necessary it is to kill hares, even though, as a " sport," organised hare drives can make little appeal.

On the rough shoot, of course, a few hares are a definite asset, and when they are wild, the finding of them and even the shooting of them can be enjoyed. But, whatever size shot is in the gun, the shooting of hares over long ranges is to be deplored. A wounded hare is not a pleasant sight, and no sportsman cares to see a strong creature of this kind get away with a leg " down," or with a skin penetrated by stray pellets. Many sportsmen of my acquaintance steadfastly refuse to shoot hares, they having been upset by the cries of a wounded one—cries that may well be likened to a child in agony.

However, hares must be shot, and they can be killed cleanly by a good performer as far as forty yards with No. 5 shot from a 12-bore. The size of the animal, and its often deceptive speed, call for a good lead for a crossing shot, while a going-away shot up to, say, twenty-five yards may be brought off by shooting over the head at a height in line with the black tips of the long upstanding ears. If the ears are lowered, as they often are when, for instance, a hare is running up a furrow and is doing its best to conceal its escape, the black ear-tips must be imagined and allowance made accordingly.

There are three definite species of hare in the British Isles : (*a*) the Brown hare, common in England and Wales ; (*b*) the Alpine hare (known variably as the Scottish, White or Blue hare), common in the highlands of Scotland ; (*c*) the Irish hare, which some naturalists hold to be a sub-species of the Alpine hare, but which refuses to breed with it.

The Brown hare averages in weight about 8 lb. ; the Alpine 5 lb. to 6 lb. ; the Irish 7 lb. In the same order of species the number of young to a litter varies from 2 to 4 (and very occasionally more) ; up to eight ; three. In the case of the Brown hare, especially, three to four litters a year are not uncommon, much depending upon local conditions and conditions of weather. Like the rabbit, the hare is liable to have more litters in mild weather than if it is faced with long, cold, or wet spells. In winter, the coat of the Alpine hare turns white, as does that of stoats (ermine) in the north, and it is in the " betwixt-and-between " stages of this change in autumn and spring that we witness the " blue " hare, the mingling of brown and white tints causing this appearance. Noteworthy, however, is the fact that the black tips of the Alpine hare's ears do not change colour, the same remark applying to the black brush which forms the tip of the stoat's tail.

There is no legal close season for hares, although sportsmen do not shoot them after February and until August, lest it be the exception of a nice leveret, as a young hare is known jumping up on the rough shoot towards the end of the " close " season, when it might be considered an asset to the larder.

Towards the end of the year, right on through the spring, hares will be seen chasing each other in courtship, the jacks (male hares) giving a rare display of antics before the does, and fighting fierce battles with rival jacks. " Mad as a March hare " is a common enough expression, and one the foundation of which it is not difficult to understand when watching jack hares engrossed in their antics. " Hare-brained " is another expression based on the same display. It is no uncommon sight to see from two to a dozen jack hares following a lady of charm, every now and again turning one against the other in battle royal, kicking out after the manner of a bucking bronco, leaping high in the air, and then rising on long hind legs to box like trained pugilists of the ring. It is said that sometimes these encounters prove fatal to the loser, but I have no personal evidence of this, although I have witnessed countless battles that were not only thrilling to watch, but which sent the fleck flying in bunches while the antagonists, oblivious to their surroundings, fought, jumped, kicked and grunted until, of a sudden, it seemed, both realised that the lady for whose favours they battled was now half a field away and closely pursued by other admirers !

I have said that while these fights are in progress, the combatants are often quite oblivious of all else than the business in hand. As an example of this, I well remember how a keeper with a little golden cocker at heel met me on the downs one day and together we watched a dozen hares engaged in all manner of antics in a hollow beneath us. For a joke, my companion ordered his interested spaniel to " seek 'em." Away went the little dog, but, as he reached the group, two large jack hares suddenly became aware of what must have appeared to their bemused senses as the advent of a fresh rival. Both hares at once charged towards the dog, and the latter, amazed at the turn of events and then considering in a flurry of thought that retreat was the better part of valour, turned tail, and we witnessed the ludicrous, sight of a sporting dog (actually a puppy of seven months) being pursued by a couple of hares, with reinforcements beginning to come up in the rear. On that day I had a very wise and experienced outsize in golden retrievers with me.

and, on the return of the spaniel, I ordered him to charge the enemy. Away he went, and I can only suppose that the madness of spring fever with which the hares were suffering, plus the fact that a narrow ridge in the ground partly hid the size of the dog, combined to dull usually alert senses, for as he approached the gambolling group, two more jacks detached themselves from it and came charging towards him, girt for combat. For a moment the dog hesitated in his stride, and then made straight at the two hares, causing them suddenly to become aware that something was very wrong. Next minute he had flashed past the bewildered and now startled creatures and was among the group, doing his best to collect a prize. At this juncture, a sharp whistle from me pulled him up and a second whistle caused him to leave the hares and return. But even as he left the group, some of which had made slowly off, a " still-blind " member gave chase for a few yards. Then, in a flash, it seemed, the madness lifted like a veil from all the hares and off they went at a good gallop in various directions, while we wiped the tears of laughter from our eyes, and I patted my big dog for his display of obedience under trying conditions.

On another occasion I was hiding in a hedge, watching a pair of partridges that had a nest in a tuft of lucern on an otherwise closely cropped meadow. The hen was on the nest laying, and the cock was feeding a few yards from the nest. Presently, through a gap in the fence at the far end of the meadow, two hares appeared—obviously a jack and a doe. As they approached, Jack put on a very fine clowning act with the object of impressing his lady-love. When within about fifteen yards of the partridges, this foolish fellow saw an even better opportunity of showing off his paces to perfection. First, he chased the cock bird, causing no little agitation to that very ruffled bird, then he approached the green patch where the hen was on her nest and carefully nosed it. Suddenly, up went his hind legs and there was a

184

great flurry from the nest. Seemingly, he had found the squatting bird and had, out of pure mischief, kicked out at her. Both partridges, now really indignant and not a little alarmed, made a fine rumpus, running round with open wings giving the hare a piece of their minds and threatening it with dire perils unless it cleared off. I doubt if this display really scared the hare, but he was, at least, a little disconcerted, or, perhaps he was now more concerned with the attitude of the doe which had hopped away and sat apparently unimpressed at some distance. At all events, he never gave the ruffled partridges another look, but chased off after the lady of his affections.

I know little of the Irish hare, but am told it is a more sociable species than the others and that great " droves " may be seen travelling in company. Our Brown hare is sociable only in the breeding season. Adults pair promiscuously, and the young become independent when a month old. The latter are born with their eyes open and with short furry coats. Whether or not the doe drops them at different spots, or moves them apart after birth, I have never been able to ascertain for certain, but it is usual to find tiny leverets at some distance from each other. Very still they lie, their coats toning in with the coarse grass or other herbage, but once they realise that they have been discovered, they cry out " leek, leek," and even grunt with an amusing show of ferocity when handled.

The hare does not burrow, but when hard pressed or unduly inquisitive will sometimes enter a rabbit's burrow or an open drain. It's " home " is known as a " form," this being a " seat " scratched out of the fallows or stubble, or " shaped " out of coarse grass, heather, or similar cover. As it lies in its form, the prominent large eyes, with their horizontal pupils, give a wild field of vision. Hares that have been much disturbed by men or dogs will leave their forms far in advance of an approaching enemy. Left in comparative peace, they will remain crouching, relying on the natural camouflage of their coats toning with the immediate surroundings. Leaving the form of their own will, they often leap sideways before moving away, and, on returning, repeat this process, once or more than once, in order to break their line of scent, which might otherwise be followed by a stoat, or some other enemy.

On water-meadows over which I shoot, hares are to be found in forms among the reed-tussocks surrounded by water, and I have often disturbed a hare from such a spot and watched it cross a flooded meadow, swimming the deep places and bounding like a dog over the shallower spots. Possibly they consider such damp positions as some measure of self-protection. Examination of these " island " forms shows many of them to be dry, but it is by no means uncommon to find others containing an inch or more of water, in which the hare has been lying. Many instances are on record of hares deliberately swimming rivers that were as wide as two hundred yards, in order to reach good feeding, or for purposes of mating.

The normal food of the hare is bark, grain, roots and herbaceous plants. Where hares feed on sprouting corn, little damage will be seen, for they wander over a wide range, nibbling here and there. Likewise a bite here and a nibble there among a field of roots is hardly noticed by a farmer, unless there are many hares about the place. Rabbits, on the other hand, feed in a semi-circle from their burrows, not venturing farther than they need, and being ever ready to tear back to their holes on the approach of danger. Thus, while a quantity of hares may do more damage to crops than a few rabbits, the work of rabbits will be conspicuous, and that of the hares barely noticeable, except to the expert eye.

There are two popular fallacies concerning the hare that deserve to be exploded. One is that the jack is larger than the doe. In fact, the doe is the larger creature and her head

186

is less narrow than that of the jack. The other is that the hare is dumb. I have already told how the young, when alarmed, call " leek, leek " and grunt in rage, and how the fighting hare grunts in battle and the wounded hare cries like a baby in distress. Apart from these sounds, there is the call of the hare that sounds like " aunt," and perhaps the reason why the animal is known as " Auntie " in many parts of the country, although " Puss " is probably the most popular nickname. The warning sound of hares, as corresponding to the warning thump of a stamping rabbit, is a grinding of the teeth. Lastly, the mating call of the hare is well known to gamekeepers and poachers, and hares are decoyed to within range by the latter with a good imitation of this sound. The process is known as hare-sucking. Happily, my travels have led me to believe that this " art " is dying out, and it is just as well that it should.

Complaints are rife in many parts of the country that hares are far more scarce than formerly, and this fact I put down almost entirely to mechanised farming, although the popularity of the syndicate shoot and the temptation to kill too many hares has undoubtedly caused a scarcity in many neighbourhoods. The old ploughman, following his horses, would often halt his team to rescue some luckless leveret squatting close at hand, removing it to safety, even as he removed the eggs of plover, if there were four in a nest and therefore likely to be " setty." Likewise the same man, drilling the corn, or harrowing or rolling the field, would remove many leverets from harm's way. To-day, the thunderous tractor pulls the many-sheared plough, the set of harrows and the heavy roller. Before this " ironmongery," in sheer terror, crouches the leveret and next instant it is dead, its poor remains crushed into the earth. This tragedy, multiplied a hundred times on a big farm, no doubt accounts more for a scarcity of hares than the poacher's gate-net, snares and " long-dogs." On downland that remains uncultivated, hares thrive, and though poachers may sometimes make inroads among them, there is seldom any seriously marked depletion in their numbers.

To-day, then, the hare in some districts is faced with the problem of existence. All the more reason why sportsmen should give it the consideration it deserves, foregoing the temptation of shooting at it at extreme ranges and beyond, and always remembering that a few hares are a real asset on the rough shoot.

CHAPTER TWENTY

The Not-so-Humble Rabbit

Rights of Occupier and Sporting Tenant—Controlling the Rabbit—Characteristics and Habits—" Stinking-out "—In the Harvest Field ; Autumn and Winter Shooting—A few useful Hints.

WHILE it is true that rabbits, if allowed to breed practically unchecked, are capable of doing great damage to farm crops, it should be realised that it is possible to control their populations in a number of ways. I confess that I have ever been at a loss to understand why so many farmers do not take advantage of these ways to reduce the number of rabbits on their land, instead of, as is so often the case, allowing them to increase until they become a real plague on a farm, consuming growing crops and valuable grass, besides destroying pastureland with their urine and playing havoc among the roots of hedgerows.

As this is a book dealing primarily with sport, I do not intend to dwell on the destruction of rabbits other than by sporting means, but, for the benefit of sportsmen who may receive complaints from the farmer that they are not doing their best to keep down the rabbits, I feel that a few remarks on rabbit control will not be amiss.

Under the Ground Game Acts the right to kill rabbits falls equally upon the farmer and the shooting tenant. This means that either of them may kill as many rabbits as he likes, despite the protests of the other. The sportsman may shoot or otherwise take what rabbits he chooses, or put his keeper, or a rabbit-catcher on to do so. The farmer may destroy as many rabbits as and how he chooses, but there are only three classes of persons (and they must produce their right in writing) that the occupier of land may authorise to take ground game. These are (*a*) members of the occupier's household resident on the land in his occupation; (*b*) persons in the ordinary service of the occupier on the land occupied, such as regular (not casual) farm labourers ; (*c*) any one other person genuinely employed for reward to take ground game, such as a professional rabbit-catcher, but there must be genuine employment for reward, though this need not necessarily be money, a gift of rabbits to the rabbit-catcher constituting reward. The occupier who wishes to give a friend a little sport with the rabbits must ask permission from the shooting tenant, who will no doubt readily agree. Most farmers are only too glad for the shooting tenant to kill as many rabbits as possible and so preserve the crops, but I have experienced cases where the farmer and his sons also enjoyed a little rabbiting when things were slack on the farm and asked the shooting tenant to leave certain banks or a certain area unshot, so far as rabbits were concerned, in order that they might have a day or two there themselves. Such a proposition should be readily agreed to, not only from the point of view of sportsmanship, but because it should ever be the shooting man's aim to keep on the very friendliest terms with farmers and those who labour on the land. Also, and for the same reasons, every effort should be made by the shooting tenant to keep down rabbits that are damaging crops, especially if the farmer has made a point of requesting the sportsman to do so. Bad feeling between occupier and shooting tenant, which should be avoided at all costs, may lead to friction of a practical kind, when even the ludicrous position may arise of farmer and sportsman attempting to " out-ferret " each other.

Now a word on rabbit control. If a farm is overrun with rabbits, a professional rabbit-catcher should be employed to trap and snare, and to do so systematically, and with no thought of leaving a breeding stock. An agreement can be made with him whereby he retains a percentage of the rabbits caught, or he may be paid at so much a couple, his employer marketing the rabbits. In this way, further damage to crops is prevented, while the farmer is in pocket over the sale of rabbits caught. Indeed, there are cases on record where the sale of rabbits has paid for the rental of the land !

Prior to the war, there was a great outcry in the land concerning a plague of rabbits and, of course, our old friends the anti-sport societies did their best to agitate for the extermination of the cony. The result was that a Bill was passed which compelled farmers to keep the rabbit populations of their farms in strict control or, following a warning by the local County Council, the said County Council on such a warning being ignored has the power to send its own rabbit-catchers on to the land to destroy the rabbits in the manner it considers best. Even the gassing of rabbits has been advocated and carried out, a form of control that is both unnecessary and causes a great waste of valuable food, for rabbit flesh is good and nutritive and its value cannot be over-estimated in war-time.

Now let us consider the rabbit's habits and characteristics and the very important place it occupies in sport. The male and the female rabbit are known as buck and doe. Apart from the more obvious method of telling the sex of a dead rabbit, it will be seen that the head of the doe is longer and of more delicate modelling than that of the buck. The average weight of a rabbit is from 2½ lb. to 3 lb.

Breeding commences in warm weather before the doe is full grown. Rabbits breed during spring and summer ; also, less frequently in autumn and even winter, but in mild weather and in light soil. Before laying down her young, the doe makes a nest of fur plucked from herself and also adds mouthfuls of dried grass collected from the neighbourhood of the hole. While a great many young are born in burrows, in dead-ends scratched out by the doe, a big percentage of nests will also be found in " stops " in the open—*i.e.* single holes scratched out in fields and meadows, often far from the nearest burrow. The reason for this is usually that there are too many buck rabbits in the colony. They unduly worry the does and also attack the young when born, pulling them and the nests outside the burrow. I have often found big burrows completely cleared of nests and young by buck rabbits, despite the plucky defence put up by doe rabbits in defence of their young. It is probable that the bucks take advantage of the absence of does out feeding to accomplish their fell work, for I cannot imagine even a strong buck rabbit facing an infuriated mother defending her young. On several occasions I have witnessed does with young drive off stoats, weasels, rats and ferrets, stamping, growling and grunting as they faced up to the enemy with all the courage possessed of a mother whose young are in danger of their lives.

Feeding does seldom venture far from the burrow where their young lie, and, in the case of " stops " in the open, take the precaution of covering up the entrance to the hole while they are away. Thus, should you come on disturbed earth, resembling a mole-hill that has been scratched level with the ground, it is probable that, by probing in the ground, you will discover the entrance to a " stop " and two to four feet in will be found a nest of fur and snuggling in it from two to eight pink motionless morsels, their ears sealed and their eyes closed. For eleven days they will lie thus before their eyes begin to open, but a few days later you will come on them sampling the outside world, and in less than a month they will be capable of fending for themselves.

Or, in paying a visit to the " stop " one day, you may discover that something has dug straight down upon the nest and that the young have disappeared. This is the work of Brock, the badger, whose excellent nose tells him, despite perhaps a foot of earth, exactly where the nest lies. A dog or fox discovering the " stop " would have followed the hole, scratching away at it right from the entrance, but Brock saves himself this trouble with an assurance possessed of the badger kind.

I have dealt pretty fully with the architecture of rabbit burrows in the chapter on ferreting. Many of them, having contained countless generations of rabbits, are real works of art. The rabbit, although it does not appear fitted by Nature for burrowing is, nevertheless, a miner of considerable skill, using feet and mouth to dig tunnels in hard ground. In stiff clay, in chalk and even in coal you will come across rabbit holes, and here you will find definite evidence that the teeth are used on ground and roots alike in tunnelling into difficult ground.

In some parts of the country rabbits appear to live above ground as much as possible, among heather, furze, bracken and other matted undergrowth. Even where burrows are plentiful, wet weather will often drive them above ground, or a spell of dry weather encourage them to lie out rather than spend the day underground. Every sportsman who loves to wander round the fences or woods after rabbits prefers to find them sitting out. Then, whether it be a single sportsman with his dog, or a party of guns and beaters, the fun can become fast and furious.

Rabbits pushed or beaten out from cover often show a strange reluctance to go to ground, preferring to run from one bit of cover into another. This, of course, is particularly the case when artificial means have been used to cause rabbits to desert the safety of their holes. There are many ways of persuading them to remain above ground. There are preparations that may be bought for the purpose of " stinking out " holes, or paper, soaked overnight in paraffin and pushed down the burrow, acts equally well. The process in the latter

O   193

case is simple, and I will give you my own method of working it, and one which I have found to be more successful than any other. With a bucket containing newspaper soaked in paraffin and a stick, I make my round of burrows, poking a piece of paper down each hole, afterwards filling in the entrance, although this is not absolutely necessary. In fact, there are often holes that can be reached only with a stick, and these are left with paper well poked down them. At each burrow, one or more bolt-holes are left untouched, and through these the rabbits leave the place when darkness descends. Next day rabbits will be lying out everywhere, and a visit is paid to all burrows and paper placed in the holes previously left open. I know one keeper who does not even bother to soak his paper in any preparation, declaring that white paper in a hole will stop rabbits entering. This may be the case, but paraffin obviously makes a better job of it. Your second round, dealing with open holes, may be timed on the day you are going to shoot, or, better still, on the previous day.

Another method of making rabbits lie out is to run a line-ferret through the burrows, preferably a muzzled one. The scent of ferret will drive the rabbits from their homes, and next day they will be found in seats in cover in the open. Some people prefer this method to any other, and certainly it works well enough.

Here let me issue a warning. Your friends have been invited to shoot and have been informed that the rabbits have been " stunk out." They will be looking forward to " big things." So far as you are concerned, you have done your best to provide the possibilities of a good day's sport. What, except bad weather, can now spoil the prospects ? Perhaps only one thing, and unfortunately that one thing has cropped up on several occasions in my own experience. I refer to a dog or dogs running loose about the place, hunting the rabbits until they have been forced to go to ground. I remember one occasion in particular when I had " stunk out " all the good burrows in a hundred acre wood, and many burrows in adjoining fields. There was little undercover in the wood and the rabbits were sitting out chiefly in and under the stumps of ash-poles. At nine o'clock on the morning arranged for the shoot, some twenty guns turned up, and it was while we were waiting for a late-comer that I first heard the yapping of a terrier and the " music " of a hunting spaniel. How long the dogs had been in the wood I did not know, but I later discovered that they had been out hunting all night. The wonder was that they were not tired by morning ! To cut a long and sorry story short, that shoot was something of a fiasco. Instead of two or three hundred rabbits being shot, the bag was sixty-five, and we were fortunate to get that number, most of those killed being shot in the rough meadows and fences outside the wood. The moral of such bad fortune is, of course, to discourage self-hunting dogs from visiting the area " stunk out," by keeping an eye on it, and by seeing that your own dogs, attracted by the scent of rabbits, do not so far forget themselves as to slip away on an expedition that may cause you the utmost regret.

In the spring of the year young rabbits will begin to make their appearance outside burrows and " stops." As summer approaches, rabbits of every size, from the " nestling " taking its first peep at the outside world, to the strapping youngster that is difficult to recognise from an old rabbit, will be found sitting along the hedgerows and fences, almost from daylight to dark. It is great fun then with a ·410 or a ·22 rifle to stalk these young rabbits and return with sufficient to make an excellent pie and perhaps a present to friends. As the grass grows and patches of nettles reach their full height, rabbits will stray out from their burrows and then, by walking out in the grass, parallel to the fence, or by stealing along the fence and sending the dog to hunt the grass and nettles, running shots will be had, and that hesitation which must arise as one decides whether the rabbit streaking through the grass is an old or a young one, is really an aid to good shooting, for it teaches one to deliberate before pressing the trigger, or before shooting recklessly at a moving object.

Under the conditions that exist at that period of the year, the sportsman should do his best to avoid shooting at rabbits close to their burrows, for unless a clean kill is made a wounded rabbit is certain to crawl down a hole before it can be retrieved, even by a dog, and a rabbit that has been shot dead, but the nerves of which are causing its legs to kick, may well slip down a hole and the kicking movement propel it far down the burrow. When rabbits have been frequently stalked, they become increasingly wary, and it is then, in particular, that the temptation to shoot at the head showing from a hole, or at a rabbit sitting on the edge of a burrow, becomes acute. I have suffered as much from this temptation as any one!

Not infrequently, when I have stalked a rabbit sitting in the grass, its head or ears just visible, the shot charge has done its work and carried on to kill one, two and sometimes three more rabbits sitting in line, but I have always hesitated purposely to try and kill more than one rabbit at a time, even though three or four are sitting close together, because nearly always one or more are wounded, a thing no true sportsman likes to see.

On downland, where the grass is close-cropped by sheep, and rabbit burrows scar the side of steep slopes, I have enjoyed many early mornings and evenings by potting rabbits with a rifle. In flat country, there is always a certain amount of danger present in using a rifle when the herbage is thick, for a bullet will ricochet on hard ground and carry on for a considerable distance and may finish up its flight by striking cattle, horses, sheep, or even human beings, who wander about in the spring evenings, picking flowers, bird-nesting or merely enjoying a stroll. On downland, it is not only possible to make quite sure that neither human beings nor

196

creatures are in view, but the steep slopes of the hills form a background that would reasonably take the charge of a 16 in. naval gun in safety.

Rabbit shooting throughout spring and summer is almost similar, except for the fact that as the days speed by herbage becomes more dense, the first " batch " of young rabbits are themselves already thinking of breeding and there are additional interests to consider. The short season for shooting young rooks passes by. Young pigeon become strong fliers. If pheasants are being reared, there is the bird-field on which many instructive hours may be spent, watching the feeding of the broods and laying in wait for vermin that have a habit of making a sudden raid among the coops. The next real change to take place in the world of rabbiting is when the crops have ripened and harvesting operations commence. As the combine, or the binder, thunders and rattles round and round the standing corn, anticipation increases as to the possibility of half-an-hour of concentrated sport as the last acre is cut. I have spent many happy hours in the harvest field, armed only with a stick, chasing the rabbits as they left the rapidly diminishing crop and raced for the nearest hedgerow, often somersaulting over sheaves in their blind efforts to reach safety. In the days when the binder was drawn by horses, the rabbits bolted much more freely and seemed less scared than in these days when the thunderous vibrations of the combine, or the tractor, seem to drive them farther into the crop, finally to emerge badly frightened only when forced to do so. Young leverets and even old hares often remain petrified in their forms, to be crushed by the wheels, or cut to pieces by the knife. Nor are broods of young game birds safe. In other days, the carter, mounted on the binder, his eyes glued to the corn ahead, would pull up his horses and descend to remove a leveret or a brood of game-bird chicks from the path of the deadly knife, both in the hay and the harvest field. The tractor-driver, however, can give little or no attention to such matters, with the result that the toll of creatures killed in the hay and the harvest fields becomes greater every year.

When the crop being cut is surrounded by men and boys armed with sticks and eager to chase the rabbits as they make a bolt for freedom, shooting often becomes difficult, but it should never be allowed to become dangerous. A good idea is to take up a stand in the vicinity of burrows for which most rabbits are likely to make. Here, it will be a simple matter to shoot rabbits as they escape those who are waiting round the crop. In the course of my life, I think I have seen more dangerous shooting in the harvest field than anywhere else, and I particularly recall the picture of an aged farmer following the binder round and round the field in his dog-cart, firing at rabbits as they bolted and sometimes shooting them almost under the legs of the horses. I admit I never saw him " pepper " any one, but the reason for this was that no one was sufficiently daring or foolhardy to get within range of his ancient hammer gun with its " hair " triggers.

From September onwards, throughout the autumn and winter, rabbit shooting takes on a new aspect. There are few young rabbits about now, and as soon as rain and wind and frosts have combined to strip the foliage from the hedges, and the coarse grass and other vegetation has withered, thoughts will stray towards the ferret-hutches. Where there is little or no game to be disturbed, or when the coverts are driven through for those few pheasants they hold, it is good fun for a few guns to get together, some walking and some standing in the rides to catch the rabbits as they run forward. Walking guns must then be careful to keep in line and to fire only at rabbits breaking back, as they near the ride where the other guns are waiting. If dogs are assisting in operations, no shooting must be done by walking guns unless the dogs are visible and the shot a perfectly safe one. Shooting in thick cover is always a risky business, for often one gun will find good walking ahead of him, while another remains behind, struggling through dense underwood. Be sure, on these expeditions, that a line is kept by watching your right-hand and left-hand man and by standing still if one of the guns has to go back to pick up a rabbit.

Those waiting in the ride must not shoot forward as the walking guns approach and must be equally careful that a rabbit scuttling through the undergrowth is not followed by a dog. Find, if possible, a stand where there is a fairly clear place behind you to take rabbits after they have crossed the ride. Under no circumstances get excited or take a risky shot. No rabbit ever bred is worth it. The life or limb of a friend may be lost through a single careless shot, or a good dog killed. These warnings have already been given in a previous chapter, but so important are they that I make no apology for repeating them.

Walking up rabbits in the open when they are known to be sitting out is also good fun. Often the rabbits will sit so tight that they will be overlooked, even by questing dogs. Scan likely tufts for seats, for a hole in a tuft of grass may mean that bunny is concealed there in a nice warm place and only direct contact with the enemy will encourage him to bolt. I have walked a meadow again and again in which rabbits were sitting out, and at each careful " combing " still another rabbit sprang to life that I had walked over or close to several times. Broadside shots are simple if sufficient " lead " is given, but going-away rabbits are too often missed, or hit in the back legs. No sportsman wants to hit a rabbit in the " scut " (the proper term for a rabbit's tail); it should be his object, in the words of an old keeper, to " tip it on the nose." The tips of the average rabbit's ears will almost reach the end of its nose. If those ears are erect (and the same applies to a hare) and the rabbit is running away at a good pace, a shot-charge aimed at them should take the rabbit in the head—a nice clean kill.

In the part of the country where I live nearly every meadow is lined by pollard willows, and rabbits are very fond of sitting in the hollow trunks, also climbing to a considerable height up the insides, sometimes even making seats on the surface of the crowns. A ferret will usually bolt them, but not always, as they have a habit of tucking themselves up dead-ends and meeting the advancing enemy with an energetic kick. Rabbits are better climbers than most people imagine, and in a faggot-pile will, more often than not, avoid a ferret with ease.

The most difficult type of rabbit shooting is probably that, when driven or hunted by dogs, the rabbits pop across runs in dense brown bracken. This is " snap " shooting *par excellence* and to be successful at it a good deal of practice is required. Yet, whatever kind of rabbit shooting is being undertaken, do not underestimate the speed of a running rabbit. Try and give your target just that amount of " lead " that will cause the shot-charge to catch it in the head. A rabbit shot at too close range, or hit directly about the body, is not a creature to admire, especially when it comes to the business of paunching it. With its stomach and intestines perforated, and perhaps its limbs smashed, it not only looks what it is, " a horrid mess," but the cook will not appreciate it and the guest who bites hard on a series of shots will feel less happy than a guest should feel. Moreover, a man with the reputation for " smashing " his rabbits, just for the sake of making a big bag, will find that invitations to shoot rabbits will be few and far between.

Of course, if rabbits are a nuisance and their numbers must be reduced at all costs, then a bit of close shooting may perhaps be excusable. Even so, it is better not to waste good flesh, and where close shooting is likely to be the " order of the day " I would recommend using a smaller bore than the twelve. I have taken part in annual rabbit shoots where the bag numbered into the hundreds, and nothing larger than a ·410 was allowed. At the end of the day, when the rabbits were laid out in long rows, it was seen that few were badly shot.

For many types of rabbit shooting the little ·410 is difficult to beat. Where game must be kept quiet, its report is not out of place, while many of the conditions under which rabbits are shot call for light shot charges, that rabbits may not be badly smashed. In conclusion, I would like to add that the rabbit in sport takes a high place, and that those who rely upon it to a considerable extent to provide sport all the year round will agree that though it may be termed a humble cony, the rabbit, in fact, outwits most of us more often than we care to admit.

Finally, here are one or two useful hints. To tell the difference between young and old rabbits when dead, squeeze the lower jaw-bone between finger and thumb until it cracks. In old rabbits this may be something of a task. In young rabbits the bone snaps comparatively easily.

Rabbits should be legged and hung up immediately they are killed.

If you have left your knife at home, by twisting the rabbit double till its head touches its hind-legs, the slit for legging may be made with its sharp teeth. That dodge is " a new one " on most sportsmen !

If many rabbits are killed and have to be collected and carried for some distance they should be paunched, after being allowed to get cool. To accomplish this operation, place the thumb-nail a quarter of an inch up the blade of the knife from the point and insert the point in the belly of the rabbit, making a small incision. Thus the flesh only is cut. If the blade of the knife is allowed to enter more deeply, the inside of the rabbit may get cut, with the result that blood and other mess will issue and soil the fur. Now insert the first and second fingers into the incision made and tear the flesh for about three to four inches. With the left hand holding the rabbit by its shoulders, feel for the stomach with the first and second fingers of the right hand and dislodge it from its hold, taking great care not to break it. The rabbit should now be held downwards to allow stomach and entrails to fall out, and the last piece of " gut " must be broken off cleanly as far back in the rabbit as possible, and the bladder removed.

Paunched rabbits should be allowed to stiffen before being placed in a bag or sack. They may be carried on a stick, or a far better way, I think, made into a bundle by threading string through their legs, and carried over the shoulders, half hanging in front and half behind.

In paunching rabbits, the livers and kidneys must be left in the carcasses, except when livers are seen to be covered with little white cyst-like spots. In this condition, they should be pulled out and thrown away, or given to the ferrets. Spotted-liver or coccidiosis, may be due to the rabbit (particularly is this so with very young rabbits, which often die off in large numbers) feeding on wet or frosted grass and clover, or through overcrowding and in-breeding.

Rabbits with their livers in this condition are perfectly good for kitchen use, though an attempt to sell them to a dealer may be met with a question or a demand that the price asked be decreased. The reason for this is that the dealer will be faced with the same question when he delivers the goods, though, with a good excuse for a missing liver, he will probably obtain top price !

CHAPTER TWENTY-ONE

Inland Marshes

Types of Marsh—Preserving and Improving the Shoot-
ing—The Marsh at Different Seasons—Daytime Shoot-
ing—Sport by Moonlight—Inhabitants of the Marsh
—Short-eared Owls.

INLAND marshes are many and of various kinds. There
are marshes proper that can only be described as bogs,
except during periods of severe drought. Dykes, rush-beds,
acres of reed-tussocks and quaking soggy ground make them
attractive spots for all manner of fowl and waders in due
season, not to mention the game-birds that find here ample
scope for relieving their hunger on herbage and a great
variety of insect life. Then there are those grazing marshes
that become marshes only in the strict sense of that word
during autumn and winter, when rainfall descends to fill
the dykes, ditches and cattle-pools and the water drains off
the surrounding high ground to flood the lush, coarse grass
and reed-tussocks on which cattle, horse and sheep feed
during the drier periods.

For the purpose of this chapter we will take a marsh over
which I shot with great success for a number of years, for to
me it is a fairly typical example of inland marsh—a cross
between quaking, permanently, damp ground and the cattle

marsh off which good feeding may be enjoyed during almost two-thirds of the year. In some respects my marsh is exceptional; it lies in a natural dip at the foot of the hills and spreads its three hundred acres in splendid isolation on the floor of a wide valley. Three miles distant lies the winding river, and throughout the county in which this marsh is situated are many well-preserved estates on which duck are reared to add variety to the excellent game prospects.

Many years ago, the marsh, being a natural hollow, became deeply flooded whenever drain-water poured from the hills, and the then owner decided to take action to prevent this as far as possible, and so add to the value of the place for pasture. Accordingly, taking advantage of a dry season, he widened and deepened a network of ditches, so that they formed serviceable dykes that would carry away the water to a twisting boundary brook which in turn emptied itself into the river. To facilitate the passage of cattle, horses and farm carts, he built here and there wide bridges of heavy railway sleepers, and at other points of vantage single sleepers were firmly pegged down to form " short-cuts " for those who had business about the place. To prevent cattle from falling into the deeper, wider dykes, barbed wire fences were erected along the banks, but the tall, thick white-thorn hedges were left unlaid and untrimmed, to provide a break against the cold winds that swept across the valley and down from the hills. And the lines of pollard willows were left to grow as they would, poles being cut from them only to strengthen the fences at intervals of time, or to form enclosures round hayricks that resulted from the cutting of the less-coarse grass on the edges of the marsh. At one point, almost in the centre of the place, two immense hedges form a lane which runs out to the middle of the rush-meadows, and it was here that on many an evening I concealed myself to await the arrival of duck coming in to feed in the dusk, and sometimes had the fortune to shoot a goose or two as these big birds became attracted to the host of duck sitting out on the extensive stretches of flood-water.

There is no need further to elaborate the picture of this particular marsh, and the details I have already given are sufficient to form a rough picture of the place. Other marshes may be similar, or sufficiently similar to enable my methods of shooting this particular ground to be applicable elsewhere. At all events the characteristics of the inhabitants of marshland are much the same, and the hedgerows, the rush-beds, the willows and the conditions that exist after heavy and prolonged rainfall and frost may apply equally well to one marsh as to another. There will, of course, be a certain variation in the times and numbers of birds seen, in accordance with the geographical situation of inland marshes and local conditions, but the best methods whereby the rough shooter can come to terms with his quarry, and when and where he can expect to find this and that bird and what he may do to improve the attractive qualities of his marsh, should be gathered from the general hints I intend to give.

Assuming, then, that the young sportsman is as keen on studying and " keepering " such " preserves " as he is in reaping a harvest from them, the spring and early summer months will provide him with considerable food for observation, thought and exercise. If a river or brook winds through, or close, to the marsh, the rush-beds and willows that line the placid stream are certain to attract his attention, either on his way to the marsh or on the return journey. And here let it be said that it is often possible, by reversing the usual direction of a walk round, to discover many things of more than minor interest that might well be overlooked if the same path is taken day by day.

It is often the simple things that count in this respect and help to mature the powers of observation and interest in wild life. A walk beside the brook will reveal fresh evidence day by day of the process and progress of nesting birds.

The blackbird's nest in the thorn-bush may be of only passing interest, yet one gets into the habit of making a mental note concerning it, even though one seldom bothers to stop in one's stride to examine it. Last week, it was in the early stages of construction, a mere " shape " of dried grass that might be the work of blackbird or thrush. Later we noticed it taking more definite form and still later a lining of mud appeared. A thrush's nest without doubt ! But to-day's fresh lining of dried grass-stems has appeared over the lining of mud, and now we know that the architect is a blackbird, although we have so far had no glimpse of the bird itself. In a few days' time eggs will appear in the nest, and when four, or possibly five, have been laid, incubation will commence and the head and tail of the sitting bird will attract notice as we pass. Eventually, young will be hatched and will grow until the nest appears overflowing with dark forms. Then one day the nest will be empty, and we may perhaps hear or see the young nearby, but certainly we shall become aware of the warning chuckle of the old bird at our approach. Such minor observations may appear to have little to do with the shooting of a marsh—we can watch the same process in our own gardens— yet it is the keen eye and the keen mind, " apprenticed " to such matters, that will be sharpened to observe and understand better the habits of the larger and more elusive birds. The eye that can quickly discern the mistle-thrush's nest in the fork of the elm, the chaffinch's lichen-covered nest in the thick thorn-bush, the yellowhammer's home in the grass-bank, however well camouflaged such nests may be, will be the eye to pick out the plover's eggs on stony ground, the redshank's nest and the snipe's nest among the reed-tussocks and even the cunningly hidden nest of the partridge under the edge of the heap of hedge-trimmings. There is an old saying that practice makes perfect, and this applies especially to the rough shooter who delights in " keepering " and improving the shoot in which he takes an interest.

In spring, then, the moorhen will be nesting in the brook and beside the dykes, their nests built obviously among the rushes, or less obviously among the overhanging boughs of thorn and willow. I have found moorhen nests high up in trees, and others built on old pigeon nests in the hedges. Very excellent are the eggs when hard boiled, but there is something else about them which is worth mentioning. While crows, rooks, rats, etc., will discover the eggs of birds like the pheasant, partridge, mallard, and plover, even though they be well hidden from all but the keenest eyes, I have yet to find a moorhen's nest robbed of its eggs, although they may be exposed to full view and with no seeming protection. What the explanation for this is, it is difficult to say. The theory has been advanced that the moorhen will appear suddenly from under the water and make a great splashing and commotion when her eggs are in danger. But against this, by no means all moorhen nests are built close to the water. Whatever the explanation may be, the eggs of the plover, which are in appearance not unlike those of the moorhen, are all too often destroyed by vermin.

In the willow trees there will be many pigeon nests, those of the ring-dove being built among the boughs, or on the crown of the tree, while the stock-dove prefers to nest in greater safety in the holes and hollows of the rotting boles.

On my marsh in the spring-time at least four pairs of redshank nested, their flute-like pipings pleasing the ear as the birds flew up and down the meadows, or sat " bobbing " on the larger of the fencing posts. Here it may be mentioned that snipe frequently settle on such posts during the courting and nesting period, although I have heard it said that the common snipe keeps strictly to the ground. With the sweet " toi-toi-toi " whistling of the redshank disturbed by the intruder, or busy with their courting flight, there comes at frequent intervals the " ventriloquist " bleating or drumming of snipe. Many pairs of snipe nest in the marsh and, of a spring evening, as the sun sank slowly towards the outline of the distant downs, I have watched a dozen of these birds gracefully flying over the marsh, every now and again diving in that peculiar sidelong glide, with outspread tail and stiffened feathers, that causes the strange drumming sound so like the bleat of a goat. It is rarely that one hears snipe drumming in autumn and winter, but I have witnessed an occasional performance of this kind, possibly due to a fit of ecstasy influenced by fine spring-like weather.

By careful observation and patience, it is not difficult to locate the nests of redshank, snipe and plover, but unfortunately those sable robbers of nests, the rooks and crows, are also expert in this respect and both the eggs and young of snipe, plover and redshank stand a poor chance where flocks of rooks walk backwards and forwards for hours every day among the cover of the water-meadows. Unless there is a rookery close at hand, the sable birds may be discouraged from venturing too often upon the marsh by ambushing them as they quarter the ground on wing, prepared to settle if anything good should chance to attract them, and by shooting one or two, or at potting at others at long range just to show them that the spot is unhealthy for them.

There were several pheasant and partridge nests on my marsh and, during the shooting season, I used to kill quite a number of pheasants, flushing them from the thick ground cover, or hunting them with a dog along the hedgerows. Indeed, pheasants from all over the neighbouring arable land used to be attracted to the good feeding and " safe " cover of the marsh, and I might have taken an even heavier toll of them had I troubled to feed them there. This, however, would have displeased neighbouring sportsmen and so I was more than content to rely on Nature to draw the birds to my ground. Likewise, especially after a flood, partridges would be flushed from the rank grass and reed tussocks and of these I have shot my fair share, taking good care of what nests I discovered on my rounds during the spring. The few mallard nests were also jealously guarded and wanderers with dogs were politely ordered to keep to the one right-of-way that crossed the place, accessible only in dry weather.

Tunnel traps were, of course, placed at strategic places in the hedgerows and I found that I killed more stoats and rats than the keepers on the higher ground. The fact was that such an isolated little paradise (call it a " sanctuary " if you like) drew game and vermin from the open farmlands, and careful " keepering " and every effort spared to prevent undue disturbance was greatly appreciated by the more desirable creatures.

How different became the aspect of the marsh in autumn, after the frosts had attacked the herbage and rainfall had softened the ground ! In summer, the cattle stood under the tall hedges swishing their tails to keep away the pestering flies ; the turtle-doves crooned from the leafy shade of trees and hedges ; ring-doves soared out over the marsh with a flap-flap of their wings and sailed against the blue of the sky. The snipe still drummed above the reeds ; a brood of mallard circled with the eager flight of young birds undergoing tuition ; plover swooped and cried, tumbled and played over the golden carpet of buttercups ; cuckoo called to cuckoo and a heat-haze set the scene a-trembling. Now, with the crispness of autumn in the air, the cattle stand hoof-deep in the mud under the once-sheltering oak ; the turtle-doves and cuckoos have departed to a warmer clime ; where the buttercups, the cuckoo flowers and moon-daisies starred the ground, only the coarse grass and browning reeds stretch from fence to fence. The pigeon are mostly in flocks, and wilder than they were in summer ; a majority of the plover have departed out on to the fallows, where already immense flocks may be seen drilling against the grey sky, one minute bunched together like a black cloud, the next strung out in a line a mile long. The redshank that piped so melodiously when the year was young, and the occasional curlew, have long since taken up fresh quarters along the muds and saltings of the coast; the home-bred snipe remain and have been joined by others travelling south with the first sign of hard weather. Occasionally, a few mallard spring from the brook or from a dyke during the day, to make fairly simple shooting, if you do not fire under them, deceived by the angle at which they rise. Only at night will they come to the marsh in numbers, there to dibble and feed, leaving for the lakes and other sanctuary as the first signs of daylight brighten the east.

And now winter is upon us, a winter of much rain followed by hard weather in the north. Again the scene changes. The marsh now resembles a land of lakes. Two big wings of water stretch away from our sheltered lane, itself almost waist-deep. Out in the centre of the larger sheets of water are many duck. They seem to know that they are safe from approach, and many of them float with their bills tucked into their feathers. Three geese, more alert than the night-feeding birds, swim close to them, while restlessly a small spring of teal flash over the marsh, rising and diving like a comet that has escaped from the night sky and is dazzled by the light. Here and there an acre or so of reed-tussocks form attractive islands, and it is among these that the snipe are lying. Tired out by travel, or all-night feeding, they may sometimes be approached to within shot, but great patience is required, for the approach must be slow through ankle-deep water, a false step on the treacherous ground causing splashing and one or more snipe, less sleepy than their fellows, will rise with a warning "scaape-scaape," to hasten the departure of the rest.

When stalking cover of this kind, through shallow water, or over cracking ice, the dog must be left at "sit" at some distance, for, although one may, with great care, avoid sounds of approach, those of the dog are certain to be heard by the birds. Nor should a dog that is at all inclined to be wild be trusted to remain loose. A dog is very necessary for marsh shooting, to retrieve birds fallen in deep water, or those that lie on the far side of a wide dyke. If, therefore, the dog cannot be relied upon to remain where told to sit when shooting is in progress, it is best fastened to some firm object. Otherwise, when a shot is fired, it may, throwing restraint to the wind, come dashing and splashing towards you, causing snipe to rise from near and far.

Let us take a typical morning of flood. As we arrive at the marsh, duck can be seen sitting out on the open water. These birds would be quite unapproachable if one was by oneself. Even if, after a prolonged stalk, a shot was fired at those within range of a hedge, the report would put the rest on wing, and it is doubtful if they would, after circling and gaining height, remain about the place. Sometimes, it is true, the shock of a report throws them into a panic, and, if the shooter is concealed, so that the birds are unaware of his position, another shot or two at mallard or teal offers itself. It is far better, however, when there is much water out, to have one, or even two friends, for then the marsh can be stalked from various points, and a shot fired by one shooter may put the birds over another. Even so, the duck will clear off after the first assault.

It is at dusk, or on a moonlight night that the best sport is enjoyed when the marsh is in a state of semi-flood. Either two or more guns may arrange to take up positions at different points on the marsh and remain there until a stated time, or until a whistle is blown by one of them, or one gun may be allotted to remain until a number of duck have dropped into feed and then to fire a shot, or advance across the marsh, driving the birds over his companions. So far as this latter manœuvre is concerned, the guns must be well acquainted with the place and the more usual flights of the birds. Often duck come in from a known direction and will, when disturbed, return along the same line of flight. The gun, or guns, ambushed at the point of the marsh over which the duck first arrive should hold their fire, allowing the birds to settle and congregate—wait, in fact, until the gun on the far side decides to shoot, or walk out into the marsh.

The ideal night for the purpose is one on which the moon rises early and the sky contains a few banks of clouds. Against a clear moonlit sky it is almost impossible to see the birds, although their voices and the whisper of pinions may be heard, apparently close overhead. Against a background of cloud, the shapes of flying birds become discernible. It is, perhaps, a matter of opinion as regards wind. With a stiff breeze blowing, it is possible to take advantage of it in more ways than one. The birds are more likely to come in flying low, and shots at a distance, their reports being carried away from the marsh, will not have that same disturbing effect of similar reports crashing out and billowing over the water as occurs when the night is still.

I have stood knee-deep in water between the tall hedges of my lane at dusk, waiting for the early arrival of duck. Among the intricate lace-work of the whitethorns, roosting moorhen can be seen in silhouette against the dulling sky. Already the snipe are beginning to move, flying from the shelter of their daytime cover to the available feeding-spots about the marsh. Presently, there are a score of birds within hearing, their harsh " talking " seeming to come from every point of the compass. Small shapes are seen flitting against the darkening sky, and one may be tempted to take a shot at them. But a shot now may scare duck that will soon be arriving, and so a natural desire to add a snipe to the prospective bag is withheld. Out on the fallows beyond the limits of the marsh an odd plover cries, and presently a small bunch of them flash over the hedge, causing one to " up " with the gun. A " browning " shot in the semi-darkness might once have been the order of the day, but now the plover (*i.e.* the lapwing or peewit) is protected in most

counties, and, besides, it is the duck that we must keep fore-
most in mind.

Half an hour passes by. It is almost dark, but the rapidly
brightening glow in the direction of the hills tells of a rising
moon. More plover are crying away on the distant fields,
and many have now come down to the marsh. It is too dark
to see them as they pass overhead, except for an occasional

TEAL

glimpse of a dark shadow as a small flock chase by in play.
There must be hundreds of snipe about, for now their voices
seem to fill the void overhead. No doubt birds from ditch-
sides, field-pools and water-meadows outside the marsh are
gathering in for their nightly feeding. Another shadow flashes
across, almost striking the hedge-top. Plover? No, teal;
the short sweet whistle is unmistakable. And now a low
harsh " quack — quack " is heard at a distance, another
answering it from afar off.

The moon, a fiery ball of immense size, is appearing over
the horizon, rising almost as one watches it. Another half

hour and the marsh is bathed in eerie light and the combined voices of duck, snipe and plover become incessant. A whistle of approaching pinions and the dark forms of duck appear. Up goes the gun, a " lead " is given to the leader and a second barrel is fired at the next most presentable target as it melts into invisibility. Comes a single splash on the far side of the hedge, even as the echo of the shots goes rolling across the marsh to be lost in the folds of the distant downs. Now all is confusion. The voices of countless snipe rise in shocked protest at this desecration of their peace. Duck call to duck in startled fear. The plover tear over the water, tumbling and shooting upwards in mad erratic flight. The eyes are strained to the background of sky, to catch the shadows of passing birds; the ears are alert to hear and interpret that which the eyes cannot see. A shot and then another shot presents itself, each time a single effort, and one more mallard is added to the bag.

And so an hour or more passes, with occasional shots offering themselves. Presently, however, the duck, disgusted at the reception they have received, can no longer be heard. They have taken themselves off to more peaceful quarters to feed—back to the lakes, the ponds and the lay-bys of the day, probably to the river itself. The moon, like a round lanthorn, floats high in the sky and the few clouds that earlier drifted in slow majesty across her face have vanished. Only the snipe and plover remain, restless and wary after the reception they have received. The dog has been sent to find the fallen and returns with the spoils, all but one mallard that swept down with a broken wing. To-morrow, we shall hope to find him. In the meantime we make laboriously with frozen feet towards where a single light flickers from the village.

Prior to such evenings and nights as these, the marsh may be shot for snipe during the mornings and for the first part of the afternoon. Patches of reed-tussocks can be walked up, or the snipe driven backwards and forwards over a hedge or line of willows. Many the morning I have collected ten and fifteen couple in this way. Then the dykes and ditches, but particularly the brook, may be carefully stalked for an odd duck and teal. On the winding brook, it is a comparatively simple matter to come suddenly round a bend and to flush a small paddling of mallard, or maybe a spring of teal will rise almost vertically (and these need good " forward " allowance) to flash away, across the meadows, turn as one bird and then come swinging past, allowing a quick two barrels. It is said of the teal that it can fly at 150 miles an hour, but this is an exaggeration. Nevertheless, the speed of these sporting little fowl is such that one needs to swing with and then well past them, giving a lead that becomes accurate only after diligent practice. Taking any such shot, whether the birds be geese or not, one must have firm control of one's natural excitement, fixing the first shot with delibera- tion and then " steadying up " and choosing with equal care the second shot. The second barrel, let off at random may, with luck, bring one or more closely packed birds down, but it is more often that a clean miss results, although a few flying pellets may wound, a happening that any sportsman living up to his principles should try to avoid.

On my marsh there were other inhabitants. Various species of duck put in an appearance during prolonged hard weather in the north. Coot, driven from their frozen ponds, would be found, sometimes a dozen or twenty, on the brook, or even among the springs that remained open. Water-rails were not uncommon, and now and again in the summer months they were visited by their cousins the land-rails, or corncrakes. Old Frank, the grey heron (often six at a time), would spend hours beside the dykes, or stalk majestic- ally among the reed-tussocks, rising with a harsh croak to flap heavily away as a shot disturbed the solitudes.

In late autumn, the marsh was often visited by short-eared owls that roosted in isolated thorn-bushes or among the ground cover. Disturbed, they would fly off to fencing-posts, sitting upright upon these so that it was difficult to identify them from the posts themselves. I have already dealt with the habits of this bird in a previous chapter. I need only add that I discouraged their presence about the marsh, as they killed several snipe, but the chief " crime " I held against them was the moral effect they had. Snipe, harassed by their presence, left the ground altogether and did not return until I had scared the owls off by constantly taking long shots at them. These owls killed many moles, but in their " seats " among the reeds and rushes were the remains of snipe and other fare and, although the short-eared owl in the south, away from its breeding-grounds proper, cannot with all honesty be listed as " vermin," its presence certainly proves detrimental to a snipe marsh.

CHAPTER TWENTY-TWO

Wildfowling

Wild Sport—Geese, Duck and Waders—Flighting, Ambushing and Creek-Crawling — Guns and Loads —Clothes.

OF all forms of shooting for sport there is none so natural, so varied and so fascinating as that of wildfowling. Nor in any form of shooting does environment count for so much. True, the splendour of the Highland moors is at times awe-inspiring, the undulating downlands have a charm all their own, even the plain and very English picture of farmlands divided by trim or straggling hedgerows and groups of trees can set the heart beating just a shade faster as a September sun shines down on the golden stubbles and green root-patches. It is, however, along our coast-line, where tide and saltings meet and where the smell and tang of the sea mingles with that of the muds ; where the water runs like a mill-race down the creeks as the tide recedes, and where far out on the sandbars are gathered the geese and waders, that all the ever-changing sky and light effects make glad the heart of man and fill it with a strange wonder and restlessness. It was Hesketh-Prichard who wrote with truth : " The shooter to whom loneliness is abhorrent will never make a fowler. Indeed, one might go further and say that he to whom loneliness is not refreshing, who does not feel exalted and uplifted by contact with desolation, had better stick to the company of his kind upon moor and stubble."

And so it is. The art of the successful wildfowler is a

lifetime study. The birds he pursues are as wild and un-trammelled as the winds that race over the sea. The twilights, the nights and the dawns are one with the clamour of the geese, the high-pitched piping calls of the smaller shore-birds, the faint rustling of mallard wings. He who loves wild sport and communion with Nature in all her moods will find them where the tides run and the little rocky pools reflect the afterglow of the sunsets ; where against the storm-wracked sky black wedges of fowl are etched, and where the plover flocks drill against the horizon.

It is only possible, in the course of a short chapter, to outline and enthuse over the sport of wildfowling—a sport that can be enjoyed by all, for many stretches of coast allow of free shooting. To deal adequately with all the species of birds, common and rare, which come the way of the fowler, to explain the many and various ways in which the shooter can best get on terms with each, to touch on the immense subject of migration, would require a volume of its own. Indeed, there are many books, classic and otherwise, written round the sport of wildfowling, and while I might refer to those of the " old masters " and to those of several well-known wildfowlers still happily with us, I feel that the young shot would best understand and enjoy *Wildfowling*, by Mr. C. T. Dalgety. This book I recommend for its simplicity and vivid descriptions of shore-shooting.

In my mind, the birds which go to swell the bag of the fowler are divided into three sections : the geese, the duck and the waders. Geese, of which six species winter regularly with us (only the grey-lag nests in the British Isles—in the Hebrides and on the mainland in the north of Scotland), are day feeders, the grey geese of the species flighting inland at dawn to the stubbles and potato fields, sometimes as far as twenty-five miles from the shore. The exception to this rule is on nights when the moon is full and the sky bright, when the birds will remain feeding throughout the night, passing out to sea with the dawn. Duck, on the other hand, are night-feeding birds, and during the day will be found resting out at sea, or in quiet spots along the shore and in the fens and inland marshes. The wader birds, of which there are many species, may be found almost at any time of the day, but the majority of them seek out the sandbars and muds, flighting along the shore as the tide rises and covers their feeding-grounds.

By the foregoing brief description, it will readily be recognised by those who have hitherto only shot pigeon or wildfowl inland, that the best way of making a bag of wildfowl is to intercept the birds as they flight to and from their feeding-grounds, or are driven from safe sanctuary by rising tides. It should also be evident that the shooter must make a study of the time the sun and moon rise and set, and of the times and heights of tides. Most important of all, he must discover where and on what the geese and duck are feeding, so that he is able to hide, or dig himself in, along their lines of flight. For this purpose, he may choose a shelter behind the sea wall, build himself a hide that tones in with the general surroundings, sink a barrel at low water from which he can shoot, or dig a pit in the sand, not forgetting to remove and flatten out the material excavated. Then, working to a time-table, he will be in position before the flight starts, and, though birds will fly high in calm weather or with a following wind (particularly if much shot at), he should make good execution when the wind is against them and they come battling inland from the sea, or towards the sea from the land.

In hiding on the saltings close to the water's edge, or at the point of a peninsula over which the birds flight, he should get a shot at many kinds of waders as the rising tide drives them inland, when they flight up and down the shore. With the aid of decoys, or by " calling," or even by taking advantage of the curiosity of certain waders like curlew by tying bits of paper to pegs and allowing them to blow in the wind, he will spend a lively time while the flight lasts. But it is to be hoped that, in his excitement, he will not allow himself to be cut off by the tide, which, in some places, has a nasty habit of flowing up the creeks and making a sudden and rapid appearance in the rear ! Likewise, by knowing the where-abouts of Zostera beds, of cockle beds and mussel scaups, he will discover where the wigeon are feeding and will watch for the direction of their flight in order to ambush them in due course.

Flight lines, as is the case of those of pigeon and duck feeding on farmlands, frequently change, and the hide from which a good bag was made yesterday, may be useless to-day, as fresh feeding-grounds are being used and consequently the direction taken by the birds is a different one.

Alternative to shooting wildfowl along their lines of flight is to wait for them on their feeding-grounds, or to stalk small lots among the creeks. Sometimes, the former answers well, although, generally speaking, it is not advisable, for obvious reasons. Far better to enjoy several mornings and evenings flighting than to drive away the birds from where they feed. If, however, a suitable hide is built on the feeding-grounds, one important point must be remembered. Cease shooting before the flight is over. By overcoming temptation and taking this precaution, birds at the tail end of the flight will come in to feed, whilst many of those recently disturbed will return to join them.

Signs to be looked for on the feeding-grounds, or about pools of fresh water are the preened feathers and droppings of duck, certain evidence that the birds are using the place. And remember always, the successful fowler, on finding certain good spots from which to flight, or at which to ambush his quarry, takes counsel with himself and swears strict secrecy, for to disclose such places may mean an influx of other fowlers, with the result that a good spot will become disturbed, if not overshot.

Sunsets along the coast defy description, their glories change from minute to minute and to the lonely fowler ensconced in his hide there is revealed something of the marvels of creation. Here, with the sun setting in a green and golden background, streaked with red and purple, all is still, except for the movement and voices of birds. Gulls are passing along the shore in straggling lines. From the edge of the saltings come the shrill pipings of waders. Where curlew, knot, godwit, dunlin, grey, green and golden plover flight; where curlew and oyster-catchers stand in ranks about the small, rocky pools; where the noisy yelper, or redshank, keeps watchful guard on the bank of the creek— here, I say, is a scene far removed from the game preserves and the inland marshes. As the moon rises and fleecy clouds reflect her light, the geese are calling out on the water and the whisper of duck pinions are heard overhead. Restless shadows flit by, some recognised by their peculiar characteristics; others merely guessed at as they vanish from sight. On such nights, with a background of clouds, passing duck, as they wing their way inland, or along the shore, may offer a shot, and as the report billows out and echoes and re-echoes, a thousand voices of protest will be raised to high heaven.

Our British wild geese can be divided into two groups: grey geese and black geese. The first group consists of the grey-lag, white-fronted, pink-footed and bean geese; the second of the brent and bernicle geese. The Canada geese, of which there are several " colonies " in the country, are an " introduction " to park lakes which have bred and increased and become semi-wild. There are also several species that pay us rare visits from time to time.

All geese, as I have said, are day feeders, but whereas the grey geese feed inland on the stubbles and potato fields, etc., the so-called black geese keep, except on rare occasions, to the coast-line, the bernicles plucking the sweet grass of the marshes, the brent feeding exclusively along the shore on Zostera or wigeon-grass.

Goose shooting has a great attraction for most fowlers, not only because of the size of these great birds, but because the sport of stalking or flighting such wary quarry appeals to the instinct of the hunter. To watch the geese skeins against the sky, to see two thousand birds feeding well out in the centre of a stubble field, is to know a thrill unequalled, I think, by any other in the realms of British sport.

And here we are behind a hedge, while our companion makes a wide detour in the hope of driving the birds over us. A shot, a roar of wings and a great gaggling of protest. Straight for us they come, mounting steeply as they approach the hedge. And now the leader is crossing to our right, a high shot, but we must take him, or an opportunity will be lost. Steadying ourselves, we give the necessary lead and hear the shots strike his plumage. But, apart from "flinching," he carries steadily on, and the second barrel, fired a little wildly in our excitement, misses badly. At the reports the startled flock divides, and, although we load quickly, no further shot presents itself. But see! The great bird that seemed merely to shake itself as the pellets bespattered it, is planing down on set wings. Down it goes, touching ground over half a mile away. There is nothing to be lost now by revealing ourselves, so off we go in pursuit, and let us hope that, panting and shaking, we eventually come up with it and that, in course of time, the cook does full justice to it—a fine young " pink-foot," our first goose !

Of duck there are many species, from the common mallard to the useless shell-duck; from the brave little teal to the merry wigeon; from the broad-billed shoveller to the red-headed pochard. There are those poachers of fish, the " saw-billed " goosander and the merganser. Among the sea duck, the scoters and scaup. A full and comprehensive list of these and of the numerous waders will be found in any book of British birds and should be studied for purposes of identification, while any experienced wildfowler will tell you of plumage changes and what and what not to shoot.

My friend Mr. J. C. M. Nichols, than whom few living wildfowlers know more of wildfowl and wildfowling, explains in his book, *Birds of Marsh and Mere*, how best the amateur can shoot and identify his quarry. His instructions are clear and concise. He writes of times and tides, of weather and hides, of guns and loads. Of punting and sailing to fowl. Of migration and wildfowling quarters.

While few young shots will concern themselves with duck punts and guns, or with heavy large-bore shoulder guns, I may, perhaps, give my own opinion on weapons and loads for general purpose wildfowling. The tyro sportsman may well find his ordinary game-gun quite suitable for shore shooting. The best all-round gun for the purpose is, however, a 12-bore chambered for 3-in. cases, but this is not necessary in the early stages of wildfowling. As regards shot size, it should be remembered that large shot has greater striking force at long ranges, and that much of the shooting along the shore is at long range. Smaller shot, however, gives a greater number of pellets in the charge. Accordingly, I suggest BB or No. 1 shot for heavy birds like geese, and No. 4 or No. 5 shot for duck. I am against the use of anything smaller, except for waders.

While writing of shot sizes, I am reminded that there is such a thing as " swan-shot." I am reminded of this particularly because I have not mentioned the three common species of swan, and that I would like to protest against the shooting of any one of them, except perhaps (and here I am asking for trouble !) a few mute swans when they become far too numerous and damaging to the food of wildfowl and do not belong to Royalty or to certain well-known Companies and Guilds. Neither the whooper nor the Bewick's swan retains its beauty or wild nature after death, whereas in life they add more than passing interest and pleasure to the mirror of Nature as the sportsman-naturalist sees it. Wild swans flying against a background of black thunder clouds, their wild trumpeting in keeping with the tempestuous elements, are a sight, once seen, never forgotten.

And now a final paragraph, on attire. Clothes for wild-fowling in all weathers should tone in well with the landscape and should be worn for utility rather than for " show." The ideal outfit, perhaps, comprises breeches and rubber thigh boots and two pairs of warm stockings. A waistcoat, its back lined with flannel, can be worn over one or two pullovers, and under an old shooting jacket with ample pockets. A light waterproof and an old felt hat complete the picture. Cartridges (preferably of water-tight brand) may be carried in a belt, with " spares " in a small bag and in the pockets of the coat. By this means, an ample supply can be assured, and, if not loaded in water-proofed cases, they are kept dry and handy. It is, nevertheless, a wise precaution always to carry a cartridge extractor with you in the shooting field, and particularly does this apply on wildfowling expeditions ashore and aforeshore.

CHAPTER TWENTY-THREE

Dogs and Dog-Training

*The Dog for the Rough Shoot—Beauty versus Utility
—Training a Puppy—Appreciation of Dog Work.*

WHICH is the best all-round dog for the rough shoot?
This question is one commonly asked but not so
easily answered. Much depends, of course, on the type of
shoot on which the dog will chiefly be used. If it is of the
kind where thick hedgerows, large patches of brambles and
dense cover, including thorns, predominate, then it is obvious
that a small, " tough " dog is required, but not one so small
that it may be expected to get easily tired.

I have handled many old-fashioned cockers that were
admirable in thick punishing cover, for they were able to
follow up and push out game at a speed that would defy the
efforts of larger dogs. It is difficult, however, to-day to find
this kind of cocker. All too many so-called gun-dogs have
been bred from parents that were more useful on the show
bench than in the shooting field. Their natural instincts
have been bred out of them, and such dogs are not only more
difficult to train, but their stamina is such that they cannot
stand a hard day's work. Highly strung and inclined to
nervousness, they are quite unfitted for strenuous days in
the field, and for this we have to thank the " fancy " who,
pandering to a vogue for gun-dogs as pets, have bred their
stock along lines which indicate a craze for Beauty before
Utility. If, however, one can secure, say, a keeper-bred dog
the parents of which were recognised workers, then the

Q

merry little cocker, or even the larger springer may be said to be ideal for the purpose of the type of shoot I have mentioned.

Although a lover of spaniels, I, personally, must confess that for all-round shooting purposes I prefer a larger dog of the retriever class. It is surprising, moreover, how a " tough " dog of this size can force its way through the most punishing cover, and, though naturally slower to do so than the smaller spaniel, its very weight assists its advance, and the average retriever is admittedly more prone to obedience and is of a less obstinate character than the spaniels.

A retriever, as its name implies, is properly used for the steady work of retrieving game. The idealist will view with pleasure the sight of a retriever sitting just in front of, or at the heel of, its master when game is being driven, and will remark with pleasure how, at the finish of the drive, it is sent out at word of command to gather dead and wounded game. In fact, any gun-dog worthy the name may be trained to accomplish this work, but all the retrievers I have owned and worked ever since I was a lad have been expected to do a great deal beyond this. They have been trained from puppy-hood to be general workers, to find runners, to retrieve in the orthodox manner, but also to hunt hedges and to face water under every condition.

In short, the rough shooter, who also attends more conventional days in the shooting field, requires an all-round dog —a dog that can enjoy a potter round the rough shoot, hours in the fens or along the saltings, a morning's ferreting, or a day with grouse, pheasants or partridges as much as his master. Such a dog, if properly trained and looked after, will become, in due course and with a year or two's experience, not only the ideal gun-dog, but a very real companion.

A golden retriever I shot over for fourteen years (see the two photographs of him in action) became so intelligent and such an all-round favourite at shooting parties that his name was a by-word in the county. He would point any game-bird nest for me ; collect eggs or chicks in a mouth of velvet, or was equally at home killing rats when the threshing tackle was busy. It is practically impossible to cure a dog that definitely has a hard mouth, but with due care a dog can be taught to retrieve eggs and to kill vermin.

In the course of a short chapter it is quite impossible for me to explain fully how a puppy can be broken into the gun and taught all manner of unconventional " tricks " that will be useful to the amateur keeper on his rounds, but the brief description of a few elementary lessons may assist in putting the young shot on the right road to training a puppy, and it may be added that there is no dog like the dog which you have trained yourself and which is steady and reliable in the field and the envy of all who see him at work.

The training of a puppy should commence just as soon as it is able to waddle. In a gentle way it may be taught that certain habits are bad habits and that a recurrence of them will lead to unpleasant consequences. Even at so tender an age, a puppy quickly begins to realise the meaning of a scolding note and when this is accompanied by a gentle cuff, it realises after a bit that it is doing wrong. And here I would say that a dog should never be punished unless it is made to understand exactly the reason for the punishment. Thus, if it has " altered the pattern of the carpet," its nose should be placed against the offending stain and a reprimand given, and the same tone of voice, the same method of correction, be used on every occasion.

It is extraordinary what instincts lie dormant in a puppy and it must be the trainer's aim gradually to bring out and develop the good instincts, praising the puppy when it does right, or when it is obvious that it is attempting to use its brains in the right direction. As a child is brought up first to understand the most simple things, and is then gradually educated in accordance with its powers of reasoning and brain development, so the lessons of a puppy must keep pace with its ability to understand and learn. To become impatient with it and to attempt to force knowledge into it before the time is ripe, is to encourage it to become sulky, or give up the effort to do its best.

Likewise, throughout the training of a dog, no lesson should be forced upon it to the extent that it may tire of what has hitherto been a pleasant " game," for at an early stage lessons should be regarded by the pupil more as a game than as a duty to be performed, with unpleasant consequences or the displeasure of master if any slackness is shown.

Gun-dog puppies, with a natural instinct for retrieving, will, almost as soon as they can walk, take an interest in anything thrown along the floor. If this instinct is lacking at so early an age, it should be encouraged while the pupil is still in the nursery stage. Later, when signs, through continual encouragement, are showing that the puppy is beginning to retrieve, master should walk slowly away and, the puppy following, he must turn round, take away the stuffed bit of rabbit skin or whatever " dummy " is used, from his pupil, offering an affectionate and congratulatory pat. If a dog tends to avoid bringing the " dummy " up to hand, master must look anywhere but directly at his pupil, walking slowly away, only his voice and back-stretched hand encouraging it to advance.

In a few weeks' time, when the dog has gained sufficient intelligence to realise the difference between right and wrong and to answer to a call, it should be taught to remain sitting while master walks away. At the command " down ! " or " sit ! " given in a firm voice with hand raised (and, if necessary, a cautionary tap with the open palm), the puppy, much as it may resent this new development in its education, should be forced to remain sitting at a given spot, while master backs slowly away, his eyes on those of his pupil. When a few yards have been covered, he should stop, still with the warning hand in the air, and saying " urr ! ", " sit ! " or " down ! "

After a few seconds he can say, " Come on ! Good dog ! " and make a fine fuss as the puppy gallops up. This lesson can gradually be developed until master is able to back twenty or fifty yards away and the pupil remain sitting. The next step is to walk away from the sitting dog with the back turned. This, again, must be accomplished in easy stages, every now and again glancing over the shoulder to see that orders are being obeyed. Should it attempt to follow, it must be taken back to its original spot and reprimanded. Thus, gradually, the dog will learn to obey, and, being made a fuss of when " staying put," it will soon get to know and understand what is expected of it.

There may be all manner of intermediary lessons necessary, according to the temperament of the pupil and its ability to learn, but once the lessons outlined have been mastered, it can be taught to " sit " while a dummy is thrown, and master's eyes, his stern voice and his upraised hand should be sufficient after a few attempts to cause the pupil to remain sitting while tempted to chase after the thrown dummy.

The next step is to introduce the puppy to a gun, and there are so many ways of accomplishing this that I think my own method may be followed as well as any other, although it may be contrary to the views of various experts and professional trainers.

Once I see that the puppy has a natural inclination to retrieve and, through constant practice, has become fairly proficient at bringing its " game " to hand, I introduce it to a bird, of blackbird size, which has been dead just long enough for it to stiffen, and an elastic band will assist in keeping the wings tight against the body. If the pupil treats this too roughly, further lessons must be given on the " skin " dummy. Once, however, it shows a keenness to retrieve feathers and makes no attempt to chew its " game," the dead bird may be placed in a low bush from which it will easily fall, and then shot at with an air-rifle. Seeing it fall, the puppy should

be allowed to run in to the retrieve, being egged on by encouraging words. A few lessons along this line, and a rifle
or ·410 may be used, although some experts assure one that
the crack of a small bore is more alarming to a puppy than
the louder report of a larger gun. With this latter theory I
do not agree ; that is, if my method of training is followed.
If the puppy shows no fear, but rather pleasure at this lesson,
it can be introduced to the feathered dummy being shot out
of a tree with a 12-bore, or thrown into the air and shot at
before falling. This procedure is then automatically followed
by a disciplinary lesson in making the pupil " sit " after the
gun is fired and of being allowed to retrieve only on word
of command.

Once a dog has learned to be obedient, it is less likely to
fall for the fault of running-in to rabbits and hares that jump
up in front of it. Most trainers use a check-cord to prevent
a dog falling into temptation, this being a long cord tied to
the collar which abruptly checks it as it gives chase, when it
is rated for its sins. A check-cord, however, is not necessary
if a dog has learned to be obedient from the very beginning,
and realises that stern punishment is the reward for neglecting
master's commands.

I prefer, before shooting rabbits to a puppy, to put up
one or two out of their seats and allow the pupil to watch
them running away, meanwhile saying " No ! No ! " in no
uncertain tone of voice. When, eventually, rabbits are put
up and shot, or missed (and some should be purposely missed
in the interests of training), any attempts on the part of the
pupil to give chase must be met with firm words and, if
necessary, a beating with a collar or lead. Patience will be
required at this stage, but at last the puppy will learn to
become steady to shot, though it should not for a time be
allowed to go out in the company of dogs inclined to run in,
or jealousy may cause it to forget itself and join in a coursing
match.

Firmness, but a quiet understanding of the canine mind, is the keynote to successful training. If you are not firm, then the dog will soon realise this and will take advantage of the fact to develop the trait of disobedience. I have heard sportsmen boast that they have never laid a finger on their charges. All honour to them if they can train a dog without occasionally administering some form of chastisement. For myself, I have not infrequently found with deliberately obstinate puppies and dogs, that one fairly sound beating, when this is richly deserved and the pupil is aware of the fact, is far more effective than hours or days of nagging. Consider for yourselves what excellent results a good whacking had on you, when minor punishments were smiled upon, or tended only to bring out the spirit of devilment !

It is only natural that all manner of problems will crop up in the course of training a dog, but these can mostly be overcome by common-sense measures. If not, advice from a successful dog-trainer should be sought. Even the many first-rate books on dog-training cannot cover the many and various traits and characteristics that one meets with in individual dogs.

There are a few sportsmen I know—a very few—who seem content to enjoy their sport without the company of a dog, but I confess I am at a loss to understand their mentality. It is not always possible to find your game in cover, or, in many instances, to recover shot game without the aid of a dog. What pleasure is there to shoot, say, a pheasant or duck over water, when you have no chance of recovering it ? What pleasure to lose, under any circumstances, a dead bird or a runner ?

For myself, I would rather give up my days with the gun than walk the moorlands, the fields and the woods without a dog at heel. As the true foxhunter delights in watching and understanding the work of hounds, so should the shooting man possess a natural joy in the training and the working of dogs. And when, at the finish of the winter's day, he returns muddy, tired but happy to where the lights are already twinkling an invitation in the windows of his home, his first thoughts should be towards the comfort of his dogs, to the drying of them and to the bed of clean straw where they will be temporarily kennelled. And when, still later, he relates the adventures of the day to his friends, surely included amongst them will be stories of how this and that bird was shot and of how its recovery might well have been in doubt had it not been for old Dash, whose nose and instinct seem to improve with every day that passes.

APPENDIX ONE

A Layman's Guide to The Protection of Birds Acts,
1954 and 1967

1) These Acts do not apply to game birds which are defined as:—pheasant, partridge, blackgame, grouse and ptarmigan. The Game Act of 1831 covers game birds, and a Game Licence is required to shoot them, but a Game Licence is also necessary for snipe, woodcock and hares.

2) All wild birds other than game birds are protected unless they are named in one of the lists of birds which may be shot. With the exception of woodcock the shooting seasons are the same in England, Scotland and Wales.

3) List of birds which may be shot and the shooting season of each.
1st October—31st January
Capercaillie
12th August—31st January
Jack Snipe
Common Snipe

1st September—31st January   Inland
1st September—20th February   On the foreshore
   (Foreshore is defined in the Acts as " In or over any area below high water mark of ordinary spring tides'.)
Common Pochard   Mallard
Common Scoter   Pintail

Gadwall

Garganey Teal

Goldeneye

Teal

Tufted duck

Velvet Scoter

Wigeon

Long-tailed duck

Scaup-duck

Shoveler

(Wild Geese)

Bean

Canada

Greylag

Pinkfoot

Whitefront

1st September—31st January
Coot
Common Redshank
Curlew (other than Stone Curlew)
Bar-tailed Godwit
Golden Plover
Moorhen
Whimbrel

In Scotland 1st September—31st January but in England and Wales 1st October—31st January.
Woodcock

List of birds which may be shot at any time of the year by an Authorised Person
Cormorant
Carrion Crow
Collared Dove (in Scotland only)
Domestic pigeon gone feral
Hooded Crow
House-sparrow
Goosander (in Scotland only)
Greater Black-headed Gull
Lesser Black-backed Gull
Herring Gull
Jackdaw
Jay
Magpie

APPENDIX

Red-breasted Merganser (in Scotland only)
Rock-dove (in Scotland only)
Rook
Shag
Starling
Stock-dove
Wood-pigeon

These Acts define an " authorised person " as the land-owner, tenant or person having the sporting rights, or a person having permission from any of these three, or any person authorised in writing by the Local Authority or by certain statutory bodies such as River Boards.

4) In general the Acts do not prohibit the use of decoys but it is an offence to use any living bird which is tethered, or is secured by means of braces or any similar appliances, or which is blind, maimed or injured as a decoy.

5) The Acts prohibit the use of " any mechanically propelled vehicle, boat or any aircraft in the immediate pursuit of a wild bird for the purpose of driving, killing or taking that bird ".

6) Copies of the Acts can be obtained from H.M. Stationery Office but amendments are frequently made transferring species from one list to another and adding others not previously mentioned. Some orders do not apply to the whole country, but only to limited areas, and the Home Secretary has powers to prohibit shooting on Sundays in any county.

When doubt exists information can be obtained from the local council or from the police.

Index

INDEX

W

Warren-making, 130, 131.
Weasels, 52, 58.
Wildfowl, shooting season, 1.
Wildfowling, 217–224 ; gun for, 223 ; clothes for, 224.

Williamson, Henry, 62.
Woodcock, 168–179 ; habits and characteristics, 168–174 ; migration, 170–171 ; ringing, 171 ; shooting, 175–177 ; shooting season, 1.
Wood-pigeon, 108.